D0603989

NBA

NBA

Basketball

AN OFFICIAL

FAN'S GUIDE

MARK VANCIL & DON JOZWIAK

TRIUMPH BOOKS

CHICAGO

THIS IS A CARLTON BOOK

Published in the United States by
Triumph Books
644 South Clark Street
Chicago, Illinois 60605

First published in the United Kingdom in 1996 by
Carlton Books Limited

10 9 8 7 6 5 4 3 2 1

ISBN 1-57243-156-3

Project editor: Martin Corteel
Project art editor: Paul Messam
Production: Sarah Schuman

Printed and bound in Italy

This book is available in quantity at special discounts for your
group or organization. For further information, contact:

Triumph Books
644 South Clark Street
Chicago, Illinois 60605
tel (312) 939-3330
fax (312) 663-3557

PREVIOUS PAGE Shawn Kemp and the Seattle SuperSonics put up a good fight, but Michael Jordan led the Chicago Bulls to the 1996 NBA Championship.

Authors' acknowledgments

MARK VANCIL
Special thanks to Jim O'Donnell and Jeanne Frederick for their
tireless research and attention to detail. And to the NBA's Diane
Naughton, Lee Newell, Brian McIntyre, Terry Lyons, Jan Hubbard,
Pete Steber and Alex Sachare for their remarkable ability to bring com-
passion and support to their commitment to quality. To Martin
Corteel at Carlton Books for making the process so smooth and
professional. And finally, to my wife, Laura, for all the coffee and
care. This project couldn't have been done without all these people
in place. My thanks.

DON JOZWIAK
Thanks to my mother, father and sister for their support and love.
And thanks especially to my remarkable wife, Rebecca, for toler-
ating the mess I made while working on this project and for providing
encouragement every step of the way—I couldn't have done it without you.

Photo credits

The publishers are grateful to the following for permission to
reproduce the photographs in this book: AP Wide World Photos
10, 11 (top), 12, 82, 86, 116, 117, 158; NBA Photo Library 8, 9,
11 (bottom), 13, 14, 15, 17, 18, 30, 31, 96, 97 (both), 126, 127,
130, 131 (right), 138, 151, 155, 156, 157; NBA/Victor Baldizon
NBA/Bill Baptist 106, 120, 121 (both); NBA/Andrew D.
Bernstein 4, 7 (top), 16, 19, 20, 22, 36, 38, 65, 72, 87, 88, 90, 91,
93 (both), 99 (both), 100, 101, 105, 107, 111, 124, 133, 139,
143, 153; NBA/Nathaniel S. Butler 27, 32, 46, 54, 62, 66, 67,
70, 74, 75, 78, 79, 84, 92, 94, 95 (both), 102, 103 (both), 104,
108, 110, 114, 115, 122, 135, 136, 140, 141, 144–5, 149, 150;
NBA/Lou Capozzola 25, 29, 31 (main), 37, 41, 42, 43, 48, 52,
57, 58, 61, 80, 81, 89, 98, 113 (bottom), 123, 128, 132, 134, 137
(bottom); NBA/Chris Covatta 21, 49, 68, 73; NBA/Scott
Cunningham 24, 28, 44, 47, 59, 64, 115, 137 (top); NBA/Jim
Defrisco 33, 40, 71, 129; NBA/Sam Forencich 53, 63, 85, 118,
119; NBA/Bill Gillingham 147; NBA/Barry Gossage 1, 34, 35, 50,
109, 113 (top); NBA/Andy Hayt 23, 39, 60, 95, 106; NBA/Ron
Hoskins 6; NBA/Glenn James 69; NBA/Ron Koch 131 (top);
NBA/Brad Mangin 84; NBA/Fernando Medina 124; NBA/Mike
Moore 7 (bottom); NBA/Norm Perdue 112; NBA/Jeff Reinking
76, 77, 99; NBA/Jon Soohoo 55; NBA/Dale Tait 51, 59;
NBA/Noren Trotman 56; NBA/Thomas Turck 152; NBA/Rocky
Widner 45, 72.

CONTENTS

INTRODUCTIuN

On and off the court and all around the globe, the evolution of the NBA now seems more like a revolution.

A game once confined to a small group of major American cities and carried most often via radio, now reaches into 27 major markets in the United States and two more in Canada, with television providing action to more than 160 countries around the world.

New franchises have been added in Toronto and Vancouver, Canada, and NBA players, once banned from international competition, captured the imagination of fans from Spain to Australia, Japan to South Africa as members of Dream Team III at the Atlanta Olympics.

When NBA Commissioner David Stern visited China, officials asked him to bring the "Red Oxen," or the Chicago Bulls as they are known in the U.S. When he spoke with government leaders in Russia they asked about playing an NBA game in Red Square. When the league decided to take the game international, season-opening games were played in Japan.

Indeed, the game and its players has caused a stir well beyond the traditional boundaries of North America. And with good reason.

After veteran stars such as Wilt Chamberlain, Bill Russell, George Mikan, Jerry West, Oscar Robertson and Elgin Baylor carried the league through the 1950s and 1960s, a whole new wave of talent took over and set the stage for an unprecedented explosion in worldwide interest.

Julius Erving became one of the first players to stretch the imagination with his performances. His high-flying style and acrobatic dunks helped "Dr. J" establish a whole new standard for the next generation of players.

And they must have been paying attention because the 1980s proved to be the dawn of a new age. Larry Bird and Magic Johnson came into the league together and landed with tradition-rich franchises in Boston and Los Angeles, respectively.

Next came Michael Jordan, who turned Chicago, yet another major media market, into an NBA power. Then Patrick Ewing, the 7–0 center with a soft jump shot, went to the New York Knicks, whose history matches that of the league itself.

Other stars such as Charles Barkley, Dominique Wilkins, Chris Mullin, Scottie Pippen, Hakeem Olajuwon and David Robinson joined in and helped turn the NBA game into a non-stop show.

Major television contracts brought the NBA to more homes than ever, widening the audience to viewers in virtually every country of the world. NBA arenas turned into miniature theme parks, each with its own attractions, and attendance for regular season games exploded.

Most importantly, the players didn't disappoint. Bird's Boston Celtics and Johnson's Los Angeles Lakers spent much of the 1980s fighting off challengers for NBA Championships. Then came the

Shaquille O'Neal dunks again.

4

were nearing their considerable potential.

As the NBA heads toward the 21st century, fans around the world are now watching the game that started from humble beginnings more than a century ago.

He stands just 6–6 and has more than 250 pounds backed onto his compact frame, but Charles Barkley remains among the most dynamic rebounders and scorers the game has ever known.

Detroit Pistons of Isiah Thomas and finally, after a glorious rise, Jordan's Chicago Bulls who reeled off three consecutive titles.

The players became some of the most recognizable athletes in the history of professional sports, their exploits and personalities making the NBA experience as great off the court as on.

And as the 1980s gave way to the 1990s, the league's popularity gained momentum. The Dream Team was the talk of the 1992 Olympic Games, while the next generation is taking its lead from Shaquille O'Neal, Alonzo Mourning, Larry Johnson, Anfernee Hardaway, Jason Kidd, Glenn Robinson and Grant Hill. The revolution rolls on.

By 1996, the NBA had become a phenomenal melting pot of past, present and future stars. Jordan returned from a brief retirement to lead the Bulls to a fourth NBA Championship and establish himself as the best player to ever lace up a pair of gym shoes. Magic Johnson came back after four seasons of retirement to show that his 37-year-old body still had the ability to run the Showtime offense he made famous. Stars like Scottie Pippen, John Stockton, Grant Hill, Shaquille O'Neal and Shawn Kemp were established among the game's top players, while young guns like Damon Stoudamire, Juwan Howard and Jerry Stackhouse

With the speed and quickness of a guard and the scoring ability of a small forward, David Robinson has redefined the center position. At 7–1, Robinson is a force at either end of the floor.

THE HISTORY OF THE NBA

It all started with a peach basket and a round ball more than 100 years ago. But in the decades since Dr. James Naismith created the first rough version of basketball, the National Basketball Association has become home to the greatest players in the history of the game. From the NBA's first great big man, George Mikan, to the Boston Celtics dynasty and the great 1980s run of Larry Bird, Magic Johnson, Isiah Thomas and Michael Jordan, the league has become an international show and one of the most popular spectator sports of all time.

The Birth of a League

Dr. James Naismith couldn't have known that his simple idea would lead to the creation of a game played around the globe by some of the most gifted athletes sports had ever seen.

In 1891, Dr. Naismith had two peach baskets nailed to a gymnasium balcony at the Springfield Young Men's Christian Association Training School. Dr. Naismith was hoping to create an indoor activity during the cold winter months, and by hanging the baskets high off the ground he sought to promote finesse and agility over mere size and strength.

In less than 50 years, however, the game came to revolve around players with a variety of all-around skills. And by the spring of 1946, the beginnings of the NBA were firmly in place. Although college basketball dominated the interest of fans in America, the professional game started coming together. Though teams had been organized and playing for nearly 40 years, the level of interest rarely extended beyond the team's immediate geographical area.

The Basketball Association of America was no different, at least in its first season in 1946–47. There were 11 teams divided into two divisions, the Western and Eastern, and they were situated in some of the

Dr. Naismith holds an early model basketball.

country's biggest cities, including Boston, New York, Chicago, Philadelphia, Detroit and Cleveland. The league even had a franchise in Toronto.

The BAA also had a legitimate star in "Jumpin'" Joe Fulks, a 6–5 forward from Kentucky. At a time when no team was averaging as many as 80 points a game, Fulks was a sensation. Fulks was the only player to average more than 17 points a game as he led the BAA with a 23.2 points per game average during the league's inaugural season.

The BAA ran into immediate problems. By the start of the league's second season only seven teams remained. Baltimore eventually was added to even the divisions, but problems persisted and no one was sure whether a professional basketball league, particularly in a climate dominated by the college style and game, could flourish. The concept needed help at virtually every turn. Six of the eight BAA teams were in the East, which shut out most of the rest of the country. And while Fulks and Max Zaslofsky were legitimate stars, the league needed a high profile draw.

The BAA got significant boosts on both fronts

starting with the 1948–49 season when four teams from the National Basketball League, which operated primarily in the Midwest, joined forces with the BAA. Suddenly, the BAA had some of the highest profile players in some of the best basketball markets in the country.

THE NBA BEGINS

And, perhaps as important as anything that had happened to date in professional basketball, the BAA had George Mikan.

The BAA changed its name to the the National Basketball Association for the 1949–50 season when the surviving teams from the National Basketball League merged with the BAA. The league, rugged and prone to fouls because of some of its early rules, continued to fight through its problems as

• •

Bob Cousy (right) was one of the greatest point guards in NBA history.

more and more stars emerged. The game itself needed refinement. The first move in that direction came prior to the 1954–55 season when owners from the nine remaining NBA teams adopted two radical, and equally important, rules changes.

Syracuse owner Danny Biasone had dabbled with the concept of putting a time limit on ball possession. The idea was to keep teams from stalling. Not only was the tactic boring, but it disrupted a game that revolved around scoring. Biasone arrived at 24 seconds by figuring teams normally average 60 shots a game. Thus, 120 shots divided into 2,880, the number of seconds in a 48-minute game, came out to 24. The idea caught on quickly. If the offensive team didn't get off a shot that hit the rim within 24 seconds of taking possession, the defensive team would be awarded possession of the ball. The other rule involved the number of fouls teams could commit in any one quarter. Now teams that committed more than six fouls in a quarter were penalized. Instead of shooting two free throws, opposing players would shoot three for every foul after the sixth one in a given period. Not only did it succeed in making fouling an expensive tactic to keep the opposition from scoring, but it helped keep the game moving.

Red Auerbach and the Boston Celtics Dynasty

Unlike modern teams, those of the late 1950s had virtually no scouting system in place to evaluate talent. When a team chose a college player in the draft, the coach or general manager making the choice many times had never seen the player play.

All of which underscores the brilliance of Arnold "Red" Auerbach. By the start of the 1956–57 season, the league had been reduced to eight franchises—Boston, Philadelphia, Syracuse and New York in the Eastern Division and Fort Wayne, Minneapolis, St. Louis and Rochester in the Western Division. Over the next four seasons, however, three of greatest players in history would join the league. The first of these was Bill Russell, a slender, 6–9 center who had turned the University of San Francisco into a national college power. In fact, San Francisco went two straight seasons without losing a single game. Back in Boston, Auerbach took notice. The

Celtics had led the NBA in scoring during the 1955–56 season, averaging 106 points a game. They had three solid scorers in guards Bill Sharman and Bob Cousy and forward Macauley. The team also had the rights to 6–4 Cliff Hagan, whom Boston had drafted in 1953, and whose military commitment was coming to a close.

But Auerbach needed a rebounder and he needed the kind of defense Russell could provide. While the Celtics scored a lot of points, they also gave up plenty, 105.3 a game during the 1955–56 season.

That Russell would be tied up with the Olympics in Melbourne, Australia, until December didn't matter to Auerbach. He knew what he wanted even though not even Auerbach knew what he was getting.

So in a move that would impact the entire league for 13 seasons, Auerbach gambled. He agreed to send Macauley and the rights to Hagan, both future Hall of Famers, to St. Louis for the right to

draft Russell.

Almost as important to the Celtics' future was the addition of high scoring rookie Tom Heinsohn. Auerbach used Boston's regular pick to choose Heinsohn, who immediately stepped into the scoring void left by Macauley's departure. With All-Stars Cousy and Sharman out front, Heinsohn at forward and Russell in the middle, the Celtics were suddenly covered at all spots.

Though the first installment on Auerbach's winnings came immediately, no one knew what was ahead. The Celtics, with Russell at center, beat St. Louis 4–3 in the 1957 Finals with a dramatic 125–123 double overtime victory in Game 7 to claim their first NBA Championship.

A year later, however, St. Louis got even. Hagan and Macauley teamed with superstar Bob Pettit and the Hawks eliminated Boston 4–2 in the 1958 Finals.

Nothing of the sort would happen again for eight years. Not only was Russell more brilliant and driven to succeed than anyone imagined, but Auerbach continued to load the roster with stars.

Players such as Frank Ramsey, K.C. Jones, Sam Jones, Tom "Satch" Sanders, John Havlicek and Don Nelson carried Boston through a league maturing quickly.

Though Elgin Baylor, perhaps the most acrobatic scorer the league had seen to that point, arrived in Minneapolis in 1958, Wilt Chamberlain in Philadelphia in 1959 and Oscar Robertson in Cincinnati in 1960, the Celtics marched on.

The Men in Charge: Bill Russell and Red Auerbach led the Boston Celtics to eight straight championships.

EIGHT CONSECUTIVE CHAMPIONSHIPS

Auerbach, perhaps the greatest coach the league has ever known, proved equally brilliant behind the scenes. His ability to spot talent and blend diverse personalities into the Celtics system turned the Boston franchise into one of the greatest in all professional sports.

The Celtics averaged a remarkable 57.6 regular season victories during the eight-year championship run. Not once did Boston lose more than 26 games in any one season. And when it mattered most, the Celtics never lost.

When the 1960 Finals went to Game 7 against St. Louis, Boston responded with a 122–103 victory. When the 1962 Finals went to Game 7 against Los Angeles, which is where the Minneapolis franchise moved, Boston pulled out a 110–107 victory in overtime.

In fact, once the Celtics reached the playoffs they seemed to lift their game even higher. During the 1963–64 season, Robertson, who had developed into a remarkable all-around player, led Cincinnati to a 55–25 record, just four games behind Boston in the Eastern Division.

Once the playoffs started, however, Cincinnati didn't have a chance. In a 4–1 semifinal round blitzing, Boston beat the Royals by an average of almost 13 points a game.

The beat went on through the 1965–66 season. But the last Boston championship proved to be one of the most difficult and required every ounce of Auerbach's genius.

Philadelphia, with Chamberlain winning his seventh straight scoring title, had added rookie Billy Cunningham through the draft. Cunningham could run the floor, jump as well as anybody in the league and he knew how to score. The 76ers finally appeared to have enough guns to shoot down Russell's Celtics.

Indeed, Philadelphia finished the regular season with 11 straight victories to win the Eastern Division by a game, with Boston finishing second for the first time in 10 years. The immediate result was that the Celtics had to play a first-round playoff series against Cincinnati while the 76ers rested.

Boston fought through a tough five-game series and was battle-tested, if not rested, when it met Philadelphia in the Eastern Division Finals. Whatever the reason, the 76ers fell apart. Boston dusted off Philadelphia 4–1 and coasted into the Finals against a Los Angeles Lakers team it had beaten before.

Still, the Celtics struggled. Auerbach had announced early in the season that his coaching career would end following the 1966 playoffs. He had not announced a replacement and early in the NBA Finals no one seemed very interested in Auerbach's successor.

But after the Celtics were upset at home in the first game of the Finals, Auerbach decided to let the world in on a secret of historic magnitude. Auerbach announced that Russell would become the first black head coach in NBA history when he took over coaching duties at the start of the 1966–67 season.

The stunning announcement had an uplifting affect on the Celtics. They beat Los Angeles three straight games and eventually held off the Lakers in a tough Game 7 for the franchise's eighth straight championship.

DYNASTY ENDS

Though the Boston dynasty would carry on after a one-year lapse, the end was clearly in sight. Auerbach moved to the Celtics' front office and the roster he had created was beginning to show its years.

Boston finished eight games behind Philadelphia in the Eastern Division in 1967–68 only to rally past the 76ers in the playoffs and win another NBA championship.

But in 1969, the last breaths of dynasty were there for all to see. And with the American Basketball Association heading into its second full season, changes were on the horizon. Nowhere was that more apparent than in Boston. The Celtics' regulars averaged 31 years of age, with Sam Jones nearly 36 and Russell 35 when the playoffs started.

The Celtics had finished back in fourth in the Eastern Division behind the Baltimore Bullets, Philadelphia 76ers and New York Knicks. These three teams had the fire of youth while Boston continued the fight with reputation and sheer intensity.

In Baltimore, rookie center Wes Unseld made one of the league's most dramatic debuts. He averaged 13.8 points and 18.2 rebounds and led the Bullets to the Eastern Division title. Although standing just 6–7, Unseld's body was packed with 245 pounds of solid muscle.

Combined with unusual mental toughness, Unseld immediately established himself as a presence under the basket, and Baltimore as a force to be reckoned with, which is why Unseld received both the Most Valuable Player and Rookie of the Year awards in 1969.

In New York, the Knicks were coming together quickly thanks to another undersized center, Willis Reed. With flashy Walt Frazier at guard, steady Bill Bradley at forward and Dick Barnett occupying the point, the Knicks were one of the league's best all-around teams. And they became significantly better after trading for forward Dave DeBusschere midway through the 1968–69 season. The Knicks, as it turned out, were only a season away from taking over where the Celtics left off.

Philadelphia, led by Cunningham, Hal Greer and Chet Walker remained solid as well. So, as the aging Celtics walked softly into the 1969 playoffs, the NBA's past, as well as its future, was there for all the world to see.

But the last gasp of champions proved to be just enough. Boston knocked off Philadelphia 4–1 in the semifinals, New York 4–2 in the Eastern Conference Finals and, matched once more against the Los Angeles Lakers, rolled into the NBA Finals.

Though the Lakers had Chamberlain this time, nothing changed. The Celtics came back from an early 2–0 deficit and won the deciding Game 7 by a single basket. The 11th championship in 13 years was the last for Russell, who retired as player and gave up the coaching reins at the same time.

"He was the greatest defensive player I have ever seen," states current Chicago General Manager Jerry Krause. "A lot of people say Russell couldn't play in today's game. A lot of people don't know Russell. He would have found a way. He knew how to win. And he would have found a way to adapt."

To this day, there are few players in the NBA who measure up to Russell as a combination of individual talent and team skills. He rebounded like Dennis Rodman and blocked shots like Dikembe Mutombo, and while he wasn't known as an offensive powerhouse, he found a way to score. Among the current generation of players, Russell would deserve comparisons to Michael Jordan, Magic Johnson and Larry Bird as superstars who elevated their teams to new heights.

The 1970s—The Changing of the Guard

After years of dominance by Boston in particular and the Eastern Division in general, the balance of power shifted almost annually during the 1970s. Eight different teams won championships including Seattle and Portland. The Los Angeles Lakers ended a run of futility in the Finals by winning one title while New York and Boston captured two apiece. Off the court, the American Basketball Association ceased operations in the middle of the decade with four teams joining the NBA.

Although the New York Knicks, coached by Red Holzman, took the decade's first championship, the biggest story of the season unfolded in Milwaukee.

Prior to the 1969–70 season, the Bucks and Phoenix Suns flipped a coin to determine the first pick in the 1969 NBA Draft. The coin flip had become an annual event between the two worst teams in the league, one each from the Western and Eastern Divisions.

But this one became one of the most important in basketball history. Lew Alcindor, or Kareem Abdul-Jabbar as he would be known later, had been one of the greatest players in college history at UCLA. With an unstoppable "sky-hook" and unusual agility given his slender 7–2 frame, Abdul-Jabbar was considered likely to become professional basketball's next dominant player.

Milwaukee won the flip and the NBA rights to Abdul-Jabbar. After the ABA failed to come up with a suitable financial package, Abdul-Jabbar agreed to sign with the Bucks. His impact, as expected, was immediate. He finished second in scoring (28.8) and third in rebounding (14.5) while lifting Milwaukee from 27 to 56 victories in his first season.

"He was an incredible player from the minute he joined the league," says former NBA player and coach Kevin Loughery. "There wasn't anything he couldn't do. And he had that shot that no one could stop."

The Knicks meanwhile had put together a team as fundamentally sound as any in history. Smart, disciplined, versatile and focused, New York had the league's best record and went on to record the franchise's first championship with a rousing seven-game Finals victory over the Lakers.

A year later Oscar Robertson, who had failed to win a single title during his brilliant career in Cincinnati, joined Milwaukee and provided all the help Abdul-Jabbar needed. The Bucks won a stunning 66 games during the regular season and breezed through the playoffs.

Boston, after a down period following Russell's retirement, came back strong starting with the 1971–72 season. The Celtics had players such as John Havlicek, Jo Jo White, Dave Cowens and Don Chaney leading yet another Eastern Division charge.

THE GREATEST SEASON

But no team could stop the last, and one of the greatest, runs put together by Chamberlain's 1971–72 Los Angeles Lakers. At 35, Chamberlain was now more of a defender and rebounder. The Lakers' offense revolved around sharpshooting guards Gail Goodrich and veteran Jerry West; Happy Hairston and Jim

McMillian, solid players, manned the forward spots, and the bench included future coach Pat Riley.

For all the dominance displayed by Boston during the 1960s and Milwaukee during the previous season, nothing could compare to Los Angeles' record-shattering assault.

They won an NBA-record 33 straight games during one stretch and finished 69–13 during the regular season. The Lakers were so dominant that they won by an average of more than 12 points a game while leading the league in scoring (121.0).

The playoffs weren't much different. Los Angeles had lost seven times in the championship round in nine years before 1972. Matched against the New York Knicks, that string stopped quickly. The Lakers knocked off New York 4–1 for the franchise's first title since the team moved from Minneapolis in 1960.

Over in the ABA, the league had discovered the one player who would eventually become its savior. After his junior season at the University of Massachusetts, Julius Erving was signed by the Virginia Squires. Erving became an instant sensation, averaging 27.3 points and 15.7 rebounds a game.

But it was not what Erving did as much as the flash and flair of the process. His dunks were thundering and came from everywhere. He slammed on the run, under the basket and over everyone, including 7–2 Kentucky center Artis Gilmore.

Though the ABA and NBA continued to talk about a merger, Erving would be the one player to eventually push the process forward.

Back in the NBA, the Boston Celtics were once again riding high in the East. Led by Havlicek's scoring and Dave Cowens' aggressive play in the middle, Boston averaged a league-high 59 victories from the start of the 1971–72 season through the 1976 Finals.

But unlike their predecessors, these Celtics didn't always get it done in the playoffs. During the five-season sprint Boston reached the Finals only twice, winning in 1974 and 1976.

● ●

LEFT Kareem Abdul-Jabbar
RIGHT Wilt Chamberlain rises above the crowd.

EXPANSION

The league, loaded with talent, expanded to 18 teams for the 1974–75 season, adding New Orleans, which would later become the Utah Jazz. More importantly, the power was distributed evenly among a handful of teams.

The Chicago Bulls, coached by Dick Motta, remained one of the league's toughest defensive teams. The Buffalo Braves, with high-scoring Bob McAdoo, improved to 49 victories while the Washington Bullets, with Elvin Hayes on board, were the East's best team.

But out West, three teams had emerged. Golden State, with Rick Barry back in the fold, won the Pacific Division and put together a brilliant postseason run that took the Warriors all the way to the Finals. Right behind them, however, were Seattle and Portland. The SuperSonics were slowly building toward a title run of their own later in the decade while the Trail Blazers had won the 1974 coin flip for center Bill Walton.

Golden State's title romp past Washington only delayed the Bullets' own championship.

After Boston won in 1976, Portland, Washington and Seattle followed with championships.

Off the court, the last major piece of business was finally resolved when four ABA teams—Denver, Indiana, New York and San Antonio—were admitted into the NBA prior to the 1976–77 season. It seemed only fitting that as the NBA celebrated its 30th season the ABA would be suffering through the last of its problems. The NBA started the 1976–77 season with 22 teams and a whole new group of potential stars.

A controversial trade landed Erving in Philadelphia, while Denver had David Thompson, the first No. 1 draft pick to ever sign with the ABA, and Dan Issel. San Antonio had high-scoring guard George "Ice" Gervin and high-flying Larry Kenon and Indiana had high-scoring Billy Knight.

The Trail Blazers appeared to be on the verge of a dynasty thanks to Walton's presence. But the oft-injured center, who had been compared to everyone from Abdul-Jabbar to Russell, stayed healthy long enough for only a single championship.

With Walton controlling the middle offensively and defensively, Portland rallied

SHINING STARS

Though four teams ultimately moved from the ABA to the NBA, the biggest winners proved to be basketball fans.

Now, for the first time, fans all over the country were able to see players like Julius Erving, 7–2 center Artis Gilmore, 6–4 scoring machine David Thompson, Dan Issel, Larry Kenon and George Gervin, a smooth-scoring 6–7 guard.

All of those former ABA players had an immediate impact on the NBA. Erving helped Philadelphia to the Atlantic Division title in 1977 while Thompson and Issel keyed Denver's Midwest Division title.

Individually, Indiana's Billy Knight finished second in scoring, Thompson fourth, Gervin ninth and Issel 10th in their first NBA season. Gilmore ranked fourth in rebounds while Indiana's Don Buse led the NBA in assists.

A year later, Gervin and Thompson finished first and second in scoring in one of the most dramatic head-to-head competitions in history. As if in memory of the old ABA and its high-flying, wide-open game, Thompson and Gervin decided the scoring title on the final day.

Thompson made his bid with a brilliant, 73-point performance in an afternoon game. Later that night, Gervin—needing 59 points—scored 63 to win the title, 27.21 ppg to 27.15.

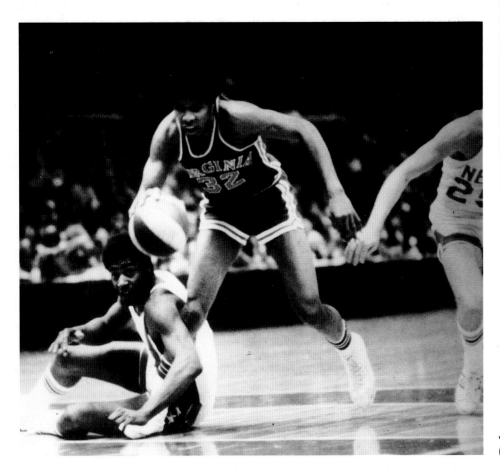

to knock off Julius Erving's Philadelphia 76ers for the 1977 crown.

Seattle and Washington, both led by veteran talent, closed out the decade by meeting back-to-back in the 1978 and 1979 Finals with the Bullets winning the first round and the SuperSonics the second.

With those championships, however, came the end of an era. The next decade would be defined by spectacular worldwide growth off the court and the brilliant play of a whole new generation of players on the court.

Julius Erving in his ABA days with the Squires (right) Magic Johnson

The Greatest Show On—
And Off—Earth

It all started where it had all started before. Red Auerbach, using a rule that would later be eliminated, selected 6–9 forward Larry Bird as a "junior eligible" in 1978. A year later, the Los Angeles Lakers won the 1979 coin flip and selected 6–9 guard Earvin "Magic" Johnson with the No. 1 pick in the draft. Once again, the league's premier franchises were headed into a decade-long battle with two of the greatest players in history leading the charge. By 1985, the NBA found itself positioned for the most lucrative period of its history. Michael Jordan landed in Chicago and Patrick Ewing in New York, giving the league superstars in its four major markets. The game would never be the same.

The twist and turn of an entire league's future fortunes hung on the flip of a coin in 1979.

By the end of the 1970s, the NBA found itself dominated by secondary markets. The Seattle SuperSonics won the 1979 championship, with Washington, San Antonio and Kansas City winning the other three divisions. The major media centers had dropped back in the pack with Chicago finishing last in the Midwest Division, New York and Boston fourth and fifth, respectively, in the Atlantic and Los Angeles third in the Pacific.

Over the next five seasons, however, luck and Red Auerbach's genius would go a long way toward changing all that.

Boston's Auerbach, as he had done time and again over the previous 30 years, made two moves that transformed the Celtics from a troubled franchise with a dark future into an instant contender.

Coming off a 32–50 season in 1978, Auerbach decided to use the Celtics' first-round draft pick, No. 6 overall, on a 6–9 forward at Indiana State University. Auerbach, invoking a rarely used rule, selected Larry Bird as a junior eligible. Bird had transferred to Indiana State early in his college career, so while his original college class graduated 1978, Bird still had a year of collegiate playing eligibility remaining.

Auerbach didn't care. As with Russell back in the 1950s, Auerbach saw something special in Bird. So while Bird stayed in school for another season, the Celtics limped to a 29–53 record during the 1978–79 season.

But the gamble paid off. Bird arrived for the 1979–80 season after one of the most widely watched college championship games in history. Bird led Indiana State into the NCAA championship game opposite Earvin "Magic" Johnson's Michigan State team.

With many highly talented teammates to back him up, Johnson cruised past Bird to the 1979 national championship. It proved to be only the beginning of an often brilliant, decade-long battle played out across the entire country.

THE CELTICS AND LAKERS RISE AGAIN

The Los Angeles Lakers, thanks to a previous trade that gave them Utah's first-round selection, won the annual coin flip for the NBA Draft's first pick and took Johnson. Boston then signed Bird and the league's two most storied franchises were back in business.

Very big business.

The coast-to-coast rivalry gave the league a boost no one could have expected. Bird and Johnson had captured the imagination of a nation during college and now they would carry on as professionals in environments perfectly suited to their respective styles. Bird, almost fundamentally perfect, was the ideal match for Boston's proud tradition built on fundamental concepts. As for Johnson, he had a nickname and a personality made for the high glitz Hollywood atmosphere that surrounded Lakers games.

Magic became "the man" in Los Angeles and the Lakers, with legendary Kareem Abdul-Jabbar in the middle, were now a team for the ages.

With the addition of two marquee names in the same season, particularly in Boston and Los Angeles, interest in the league exploded. And the players didn't disappoint.

The Lakers won the first championship of the Magic era with a dramatic Game 6 victory over Philadelphia in 1980. Johnson, forced to play center after Abdul-Jabbar was injured in Game 5, scored 42 points, grabbed 15 rebounds and handed out seven assists in a stunning 123–107 victory over the 76ers and Julius Erving at Philadelphia.

While Johnson had been solid during the regular season, nothing marked his legend like that championship performance. Bird, however, edged Johnson for Rookie of the Year by leading the Celtics to a 61–21 record and a Division title.

"Magic was the only player who could take three shots and still dominate a game," Erving said later.

Indeed, Magic and Bird went on to dominate the first half of the decade, with the Celtics winning their first title in 1981. And once more, Auerbach was in the middle of it all.

Prior to the season, Auerbach sent the No. 1 pick in the draft, which the Celtics had acquired in a trade, plus the No. 15 choice to Golden State for center Robert Parish and rights to the No. 3 pick, which turned out to be Kevin McHale. With Cedric

Maxwell occupying the forward spot opposite Bird, Boston rolled.

The Celtics rallied past Philadelphia in the Eastern Conference Finals before dismissing Houston for the 1981 title.

TWO GREAT TEAMS

For Bird and Johnson, the real showdown didn't come until 1984. Erving's 76ers, including center Moses Malone, made back-to-back Finals appearances in 1982 and 1983 against the Lakers, with each team gaining a championship.

But it was the 1983–84 season that really kick-started professional basketball into a whole new gear. The high-scoring Denver Nuggets, coached by Doug Moe, led the league in scoring by averaging an amazing 123.7 points per game. Included in the Nuggets' season-long sprint was one of the more remarkable games in NBA history.

Matched against the Detroit Pistons, Denver scored 184 points and still managed to lose. The Pistons, led by Isiah Thomas, scored 186 and won in triple overtime in the highest scoring game of all time.

Elsewhere, the heavyweight bout everyone wanted to see slowly started to form. Boston breezed through the Eastern Conference and the Lakers did the same in the West.

For the first time since college, Bird and Johnson faced one another with a championship on the line as the 1984 Finals unfolded. This time, however, Bird found a measure of revenge.

And he had plenty of help.

One more move by Auerbach solidified the roster and set the process in motion. The Celtics acquired guard Dennis Johnson, a defensive specialist and former All-Star, in a steal of a deal with Phoenix before the season.

The Lakers, having gained James Worthy in the 1982 NBA Draft, were just as loaded with talent. So when the two teams opened the Finals in Boston, the eyes of an international audience were fixed on them.

The series embodied all the elements that had turned the NBA into the hottest professional sports league in the world. The three-point shot, an ABA feature instituted prior to the 1979–80 season,

proved to be an exciting weapon in crunch time.

There were blowout victories by both teams, two dramatic overtime games and an even more compelling Game 7 showdown inside fabled Boston Garden. When it ended, Bird was named the Finals' Most Valuable Player and the NBA, already expanding rapidly beyond the United States, hit another new high in fan interest.

THE JORDAN PHENOMENON

As it turned out, the 1984 Finals were only the beginning. Chicago, using the No. 3 pick in the 1984 Draft, selected Michael Jordan in a move that rocked the record books and changed history.

For the second straight season Houston gained the No. 1 pick in the draft and selected a center. This time, the Rockets landed Hakeem Olajuwon. With 7–4 Ralph Sampson arriving the previous season, Olajuwon completed the "Twin Towers" in Houston.

Meanwhile, Portland decided to gamble with the No. 2 choice. The Trail Blazers had Clyde Drexler on their roster and desperately needed a center. So instead of taking Jordan, Portland chose 7–1 center Sam Bowie, who had missed two entire college seasons with leg injuries. Unfortunately for the Trail Blazers, Bowie's problems weren't behind him. Bowie missed an average of nearly 55 games a season during his five years in Portland.

With Jordan, the Bulls couldn't have been happier. He pumped life into a franchise that was near collapse and turned the cold and empty Chicago Stadium into one of the loudest arenas in all of sports. He also helped turn the league into a marketing phenomenon.

Jordan's shoe and apparel deal with Nike established a whole new commercial presence for professional athletes. Jordan, unlike Bird, Johnson or Erving before him, had a personalized shoe that sold millions of pairs before the 1984–85 season ended.

Jordan finished third in the league in scoring behind New York's Bernard King and Bird, averaging 28.2 points. More importantly for the league, Jordan turned

"SHOWTIME" IN LOS ANGELES

Hollywood couldn't have made a better casting call. When the Los Angeles Lakers decided to change coaches 11 games into the 1981–82 season they called on Pat Riley, a former player and one of the most intense competitors the game had ever known.

Riley had been a teammate of Lakers General Manager Jerry West and was a reserve on the 1971–72 Lakers team that won 33 straight games. So Riley, like his star Magic Johnson, knew how to win.

With slicked-back hair, a wardrobe full of Italian suits and a style all his own, Riley became the perfect complement to Johnson's wide-eyed enthusiasm. Riley turned the Lakers into an end-to-end attack, the offense quickly becoming known as "Showtime" for all the points it scored.

When the roster changed later, Riley went back to a low-post attack utalizing Johnson and Kareem Abdul-Jabbar. The Lakers also played solid defense when it mattered most and executed with precision.

Riley left Los Angeles following the 1989–90 season, having guided the Lakers to four championships and seven trips to the Finals in eight years.

the Bulls into a wondrous road show despite an otherwise ragged roster.

The Bulls finished third in the Central Division and reached the playoffs for only the second time in eight years. Off the court, Jordan turned into a household name with major marketing and advertising deals covering everything from soft drinks to fast food and automobiles.

"He's the real thing, no question," said Kevin Loughery, Jordan's first NBA coach. "He understands the entire game, on and off the court. No one knows how good this kid is going to be. He's a killer. This guy will be one of the greatest players to ever play the game if he stays healthy."

Meanwhile another Lakers-Celtics championship showdown ended with the title going back to Los Angeles. But not for long.

The Celtics added the often-injured veteran center Bill Walton for the 1985–86 season and came within two games of the regular-season victory record. Boston finished 67–15 and roared into the Finals against Houston's towering frontline of 7–foot Olajuwon, 7–4 Sampson and 6–8 Rodney McCray.

First, however, Boston had to dismiss Jordan's pesky Bulls. Jordan had missed all but 18 games of the regular season due

Boston Celtics' Larry Bird

to a broken foot. He returned for the first round of the playoffs and put on one of the greatest one-man shows in history.

Playing against the eventual champs with a thin supporting cast, Jordan bombed Dennis Johnson and the Celtics for 49 points in a Game 1 loss. Then, before a national television audience on a warm Sunday afternoon, Jordan exploded for 63 points and carried the Bulls into double overtime before the Celtics prevailed. Although Boston went on to sail through the Eastern Conference playoffs, Bird had seen more than enough of Jordan.

"Maybe it was God disguised as Michael Jordan," quipped Bird after the Game 2 scare, the highest scoring playoff performance in history.

THE LOTTERY

Houston's ability to land consecutive No. 1 picks led to the creation of the lottery for the 1985 Draft. And that's when the final piece of the puzzle fell in place for the NBA. New York, the league's primary media market, had finished 23-59 and needed help. More specifically, the New York market needed a star. And they got one when the Knicks ended up with the No. 1 pick and landed 7–0 center Patrick Ewing.

For the league, the circle was virtually complete. With Johnson in Los Angeles, Bird in Boston, Jordan in Chicago and Ewing in New York, the NBA became an even more lucrative television draw. On the marketing side, the league was moving outside the United States and into countries all over the world with sales of league merchandise spiraling.

"This is the best game in sports," said former Bulls Coach Stan Albeck at the time. "You have everything. The game is fast, the players are incredibly skilled and going to an NBA arena is fun. The whole thing is entertainment."

It wasn't until the 1987–88 season that a slow changing of the guard started to take place. Detroit, with a tough and disciplined lineup keyed by Thomas, finally knocked Boston out of the playoffs and reached the Finals. In terms of championships, the Bird era ended when the Pistons closed out the Eastern Conference Finals with a 4–2 decision over the Celtics in 1988.

Although Johnson helped the Lakers rally to a 4–3 victory over Detroit in the 1988 NBA Finals, his championship dreams ended as well. The Lakers had become the first team since the Celtics in 1968 and 1969 to win consecutive championships.

But the pages were turning. Kareem Abdul-Jabbar retired the following season after 20 brilliant seasons and 44,149 points.

"It couldn't have been any better," said Abdul-Jabbar. "Not when I can remember growing up on the streets of Manhattan and hoping I got to play one pro season. I outlasted everybody. I got to play with the greats of the game. I realized all my professional goals."

The times, as evidenced by the Pistons' 4–0 pasting of the Lakers in the 1989 Finals, were indeed changing.

Nowhere was that more evident than in Detroit. Known for their rough and tumble defense, the Pistons made a third straight trip to the championship round in 1990 after yet another bruising Eastern Conference playoff match with Jordan's Bulls.

With Thomas leading the Pistons' charge, Detroit knocked off Portland for a second straight championship. Like the Lakers before them, the Pistons felt they had left their mark by winning two in a row. But unlike the Lakers, the run came to a close quickly.

With solid support in Scottie Pippen, Horace Grant and Bill Cartwright and the steady leadership of Coach Phil Jackson behind him, Jordan guided the Bulls to the promised land in 1991. Chicago won 61 regular season games, a franchise record, and then marched through the playoffs.

The Bulls pounded Charles Barkley's Philadelphia 76ers 4–1, then crushed the arch-rival Pistons 4–0 before knocking off Johnson's Lakers 4–1 in the 1991 Finals. As it turned out, the league would never be the same. In a stunning development prior to the 1991–92 season, Johnson announced he had HIV and would retire from basketball.

Though he immediately went to work raising money and awareness of HIV, the basketball world shook. Johnson, one of the classiest players sport had ever known, left with five championships rings and nine trips to the Finals. His smile and enthusiasm had turned a game into entertainment and his ability had turned the Lakers into a remarkable end-to-end show.

"Describing Earvin Johnson is more complicated than one might guess because the man is more complicated than he at first seems," says Abdul-Jabbar. "The whole world knows about his sense of showmanship and his flair for the spectacular, but the inner man, the fierce competitor with the iron will to win, is often concealed by the smile and the easy demeanor."

As Johnson left the game, Bird limped on behind him. Though Boston remained among the East's strongest teams, Bird missed 45 games during the 1991–92 season due to injury.

THE BULLS' ERA

The future suddenly moved to Chicago. With Jordan winning his sixth straight scoring title and the roster staying healthy, the Bulls sprinted to a 67–15 regular season record. But they didn't stop there. After rolling through the East on their way to the Finals, the Bulls upended Portland with a dramatic fourth-quarter comeback in Game 6 at Chicago Stadium.

"Can they win three in a row?" Magic Johnson considered the question. "They could, but I don't know," said Johnson. "If they thought winning two in a row was tough winning three is even harder. I know. I tried."

Johnson flirted briefly with a comeback—he remained a key member of the gold medal winning Dream Team, and Bird's sore back forced him to retire.

Phoenix pulled off a massive trade prior to the 1992–93 season, dealing three players to Philadelphia for Charles Barkley. The New York Knicks added Charles Smith and Doc Rivers, and coach Pat Riley, who had won four titles with the Lakers.

But Chicago continued to roll. Jordan won his seventh straight scoring title to match

OPPOSITE Michael Jordan sails in for another slam. BELOW Hakeem Olajuwon lifts another jump hook.

Wilt Chamberlain's league record. In the playoffs, Chicago defeated the Knicks to win the Eastern Conference title. In the 1993 Finals, Jordan again came through against Barkley, as Chicago became the first team in 27 years to win three consecutive titles.

When Jordan retired for 17 months until his comeback in March 1995, the balance of power shifted toward the West.

Barkley was in Phoenix, David Robinson in San Antonio, Drexler in Portland, Shawn Kemp in Seattle and Olajuwon in Houston. While many of those players had been in place for years, the real change came in their supporting casts. Nowhere was that more true than in Houston.

Matched against the rugged New York Knicks in the 1994 Finals, Houston became the first Western Conference team other than the Los Angeles Lakers to win the title since 1978.

In February 1995, the Rockets swung a deal with Portland to reunite Olajuwon and Drexler, but for the regular season at least, the best team in Texas was San Antonio, led by David Robinson, who was named the league's MVP.

The Rockets became the first team to defeat four 50-win teams in one playoff and capped their title run with a four-game sweep of Orlando in the NBA Finals.

With Jordan back on top of his game in 1995–96, the Bulls embarked on one of the greatest seasons in the history of sports. Chicago's regular-season 72–10 record eclipsed the 69–13 mark posted by the 1971–72 Lakers. By the time the Bulls were done demolishing their competition in the playoffs, the team had amassed a combined 87–13 record for the regular season and playoffs. Jordan won a slew of awards: regular-season MVP, All-Star Game MVP and NBA Finals MVP—and don't forget his spot on the first team of the NBA All-Defense squad.

The 1995–96 Chicago Bulls may be remembered by some as the NBA's best team ever, while Jordan has certainly cemented his reputation as the most magnificent of all NBA stars.

THE NBA FINALS

YEAR	WINNER	SERIES	LOSER
1947	Philadelphia	4–1	Chicago
1948	Baltimore	4–2	Philadelphia
1949	Minneapolis	4–2	Washington
1950	Minneapolis	4–2	Syracuse
1951	Rochester	4–3	New York
1952	Minneapolis	4–3	New York
1953	Minneapolis	4–1	New York
1954	Minneapolis	4–3	Syracuse
1955	Syracuse	4–3	Fort Worth
1956	Philadelphia	4–1	Fort Worth
1957	Boston	4–3	St. Louis
1958	St. Louis	4–2	Boston
1959	Boston	4–0	Minneapolis
1960	Boston	4–3	St. Louis
1961	Boston	4–1	St. Louis
1962	Boston	4–3	Los Angeles
1963	Boston	4–2	Los Angeles
1964	Boston	4–1	San Francisco
1965	Boston	4–1	Los Angeles
1966	Boston	4–3	Los Angeles
1967	Philadelphia	4–2	San Francisco
1968	Boston	4–2	Los Angeles
1969	Boston	4–3	Los Angeles
1970	New York	4–3	Los Angeles
1971	Milwaukee	4–0	Baltimore
1972	Los Angeles	4–1	New York
1973	New York	4–1	Los Angeles
1974	Boston	4–3	Milwaukee
1975	Golden State	4–0	Washington
1976	Boston	4–2	Phoenix
1977	Portland	4–2	Philadelphia
1978	Washington	4–3	Seattle
1979	Seattle	4–1	Washington
1980	Los Angeles	4–2	Philadelphia
1981	Boston	4–2	Houston
1982	Los Angeles	4–2	Philadelphia
1983	Philadelphia	4–0	Los Angeles
1984	Boston	4–2	Los Angeles Lakers
1985	Los Angeles Lakers	4–2	Boston
1986	Boston	4–2	Houston
1987	Los Angeles Lakers	4–2	Boston
1988	Los Angeles Lakers	4–3	Detroit
1989	Detroit	4–0	Los Angeles Lakers
1990	Detroit	4–1	Portland
1991	Chicago	4–1	Los Angeles Lakers
1992	Chicago	4–2	Portland
1993	Chicago	4–2	Phoenix
1994	Houston	4–3	New York
1995	Houston	4–0	Orlando
1996	Chicago	4–2	Seattle

THE TEAMS

For all the individual demands, basketball has always revolved around the rhythm of a team. From the beginning the NBA has been identified by its teams, those great and those in pursuit of greatness.

The record books are full of names and numbers, superstars and stats. Individuals win scoring titles, rebounding titles and block all the shots. They pass out assists and lead the league in steals. But all of them operate within the context of a team. And the greatest of those teams — the Boston Celtics, Los Angeles Lakers and Chicago Bulls — managed to combine diverse individual talents into a singular battle plan.

In the 1950s, every NBA team chased the Minneapolis Lakers. But for all George Mikan's brilliance, not even he could have carried the Lakers to championship after championship by himself. When the Celtics came together under the guidance of Arnold "Red" Auerbach, they came together as a cohesive unit with stars at virtually every position. The Los Angeles Lakers, with Magic Johnson leading the charge in the 1980s, relied on a selfless approach that mirrored that of Auerbach's Celtics. Even with Michael Jordan, perhaps the greatest player to ever play the game, the Chicago Bulls didn't win a single title until Scottie Pippen, Horace Grant and others filled in around him. From East to West, NBA teams have fought to create their own history, each of them traveling the same road in search of championships.

Teammates: Scottie Pippen and Michael Jordan

ATLANTA HAWKS

TM
© 1994 NBAP

Changing of The Guard

For many of its early NBA years, Atlanta was a franchise on the move. The Hawks played in Moline, Milwaukee and St. Louis before landing in Atlanta. The common thread in all those stops has been the presence of high-scoring forwards like Bob Pettit, Dominique Wilkins and Danny Manning. But now the Hawks rely on a pair of flashy guards, Mookie Blaylock and Steve Smith and center Dikembe Mutombo.

Few NBA teams have had as many lives as the Atlanta Hawks. And few have had a more colorful past. Though blessed with a rich history that includes some of the league's most noted players and coaches — Arnold "Red" Auerbach coached the team for most of the 1949–50 season, its first in the NBA — Atlanta spent its early years moving through the Midwest in search of a home.

The Hawks made their NBA debut in 1949, coming from the old NBL as the Tri-City Blackhawks. They moved to Milwaukee two years later and legendary coach Red Holzman, who would become one of the most successful leaders in history while running the New York Knicks, eventually came on and guided the Hawks

Mookie Blaylock soars over Scottie Pippen.

through the first of many difficult transitions. Holzman actually started out as a player/coach for the Hawks, but neither his playing nor his coaching could pull the team above the .500 mark.

Then the Hawks got a break. Though the struggle would continue, the 1954 NBA Draft produced one of the game's greatest players. Bob Pettit, a brilliant scorer and perhaps the greatest forward of his era, arrived from Louisiana State University. Not even Pettit's star power, however, could keep fan interest in Milwaukee.

So owner Ben Kerner moved the Hawks, complete with Pettit and Holtzman, to St. Louis where the franchise flourished. But not before the Hawks participated in one of the most famous trades in NBA history. In April, 1956, the Hawks sent their first-round draft choice to Boston for Ed Macauley and Cliff Hagan. Though Macauley and Hagan became Hall of Famers, Boston ended up getting the better of the deal. That first-round pick ended up being Bill Russell, who would lead the Celtics to a remarkable 11 NBA titles.

And the first of those came at the expense of the Hawks. Boston beat St. Louis for the 1957 NBA title. But a year later, with Pettit leading the way, the Hawks won their first and only championship by downing Russell's Celtics. Boston would win the next eight titles while the Hawks remained strong, but never quite good enough.

The team eventually moved again, this time to Atlanta in 1968. The next great wave came during the mid 1980s when Dominique Wilkins, one of the most exciting players ever, became the team's leading

ROLL OF HONOR

Conference/Division	Eastern/Central			
First NBA year	1949-50			
Home Arena details	The Omni (built 1972, capacity 16,510)			
Former cities/nicknames	Tri-Cities Blackhawks (1949-51), Milwaukee Hawks (1951-55), St. Louis Hawks (1955-68)			
NBA Championships	1958			
Playing Record	G	W	L	Pct
Regular Season	3714	1884	1830	.507
Playoffs (Series 18-32)	246	109	137	.443

LENNY WILKENS
A Coach's Coach

Lenny Wilkens always played the game as if he were a coach on the court.

He displayed an ability to break down defenses as evidenced by a 15-year career that included nine All-Star Game appearances. Wilkens was named player/coach at Seattle in 1969, and coached the team for three seasons.

Wilkens eventually continued his playing career at Cleveland and then Portland, where he again became player/coach before retiring as a player in 1975.

He returned to Seattle and led the SuperSonics into the NBA Finals two consecutive seasons, the second of which produced the franchise's first championship in 1979.

Wilkens then moved to Atlanta where he established himself as the most successful coach in NBA history. Through the 1995–96 season, Wilkens' teams had won 1,014 games, 76 more than legendary Boston Coach Arnold "Red" Auerbach.

scorer. Wilkins, combined with players such as Kevin Willis, Tree Rollins and Glenn "Doc" Rivers, led a spirited run during the mid and late 1980s, but teams like Boston and Detroit kept them from reaching the NBA Finals. Despite four straight 50-win seasons, the Hawks could never break out of the crowded Eastern Conference playoff picture.

Coaching great Lenny Wilkens took the Hawks' helm in 1993 and rebuilt the team in his image with a team-oriented style based on outstanding guard play. Under his guidance, point guard Mookie Blaylock and shooting guard Steve Smith have become one of the NBA's top backcourt duos. The addition of versatile forward Christian Laettner and shot-blocking center Dikembe Mutombo give Lenny Wilkens two quality big men to build the Hawks' future around.

Top Two: Steve Smith (left) and Mookie Blaylock.

Basketball's Greatest Franchise

No team in the history of professional sports in America dominated more completely than the Boston Celtics of the late 1950s and 1960s. With a legendary coach in Arnold "Red" Auerbach on the sidelines and Bill Russell, perhaps the greatest big man ever to play the game, playing center, the Celtics won 11 championships in 13 years including an NBA record eight straight. Boston has won more regular season games and postseason titles than any team in NBA history.

By the time Arnold "Red" Auerbach turned over the day-to-day operations of the Boston Celtics, no one doubted the genius of the NBA's most successful coach.

As a coach, Auerbach presided over the greatest dynasty in the history of professional sports in America. His Celtics won nine championships including a stunning eight straight during the late 1950s and early 1960s. But that was only part of Auerbach's contribution to Boston's storied history.

His greatest attribute might have been making deals and evaluating talent. The first of three franchise-shaking moves came prior to the 1956–57 season when Auerbach traded veteran stars Ed Macauley and Cliff Hagan to St. Louis for the Hawks'

Dynamic Duo: Bill and "Red" celebrate!

first-round pick in the 1956 Draft.

The player Auerbach wanted was 6–10 center Bill Russell. He also selected K.C. Jones and made Tommy Heinsohn a territorial pick. A year later, with his first pick, Auerbach added shooting guard Sam

Jones. These eventual Hall of Famers helped turn Boston into a dynasty.

During the 1960s, Auerbach continued to build the team through the draft. In 1962, following the Celtics fourth straight title, Boston selected John Havlicek in the first round. Following the 1965–66 season, Auerbach turned the coaching duties over to Russell, who became the NBA's first black head coach. Russell's teams won two more titles in his three seasons in the dual role of player/coach.

Boston won two more titles in the 1970s with Heinsohn coaching a team dominated by Havlicek and Dave Cowens. But just as the Celtics appeared headed for an extended lull following a sub-.500 season in 1977–78, Auerbach made another round of off-court moves that would define yet another era.

Auerbach used the team's first-round draft pick to select Larry Bird. It was a gutsy move, since Bird wasn't eligible to join the Celtics for a year. It was also the second great move of Auerbach's career. Although the Celtics suffered another losing season waiting for Bird's arrival, he would prove to be well worth the wait.

With another high draft pick, Auerbach made his third franchise-changing move. He traded two first-round picks to Golden State for center Robert Parish and the No. 3 pick overall, which Auerbach then used to select Kevin McHale. Auerbach eventually

ROLL OF HONOR

Conference/Division	Eastern/Atlantic			
First NBA year	1946-47			
Home Arena details	FleetCenter (built 1995, capacity 18,600)			
Former cities/nicknames	None			
NBA Championships	1957, 1959, 1960, 1961, 1962, 1963, 1964, 1965,			
	1966, 1968, 1969, 1974, 1976, 1981, 1984, 1986			

	G	W	L	Pct
Playing Record				
Regular Season	3883	2421	1462	.623
Playoffs (Series 63-25)	461	272	189	.590

★ ★ ★ ★ ★ ★ ★ ★ ★ ★ ★ ★ ★

RED AUERBACH
A Basketball Genius

If Arnold "Red" Auerbach had only coached, he would be remembered as one of the NBA's true legends.

But Auerbach did much more than that during a career that started in the 1940s and continues into the 1990s. As coach, then General Manager, Auerbach knew exactly the kind of player that could make it in the NBA.

Auerbach shipped two future Hall of Fame players to St. Louis for the rights to the Hawks' first pick in the 1956 Draft. Auerbach then used that pick to select Bill Russell, who would turn Auerbach's gamble into a monumental payoff.

With Auerbach coaching and managing the team's roster, Boston won nine NBA championships in 10 years, including a remarkable string of eight straight.

Auerbach moved to the front office following the 1965–66 season. But his moves help produce seven additional championships.

And at the end of all of them, Auerbach could be found lighting a gigantic "victory cigar," which became as much a symbol of the Celtics' success as the man himself.

landed guards Dennis Johnson and Danny Ainge in separate deals, all of which made Boston the Eastern Conference's dominant team yet again during the 1980s. The Bird era produced three championships and five more trips to the NBA Finals.

And the dominance might have continued had tragedy not dealt the franchise two major blows. Young Len Bias, considered the link to yet another golden era, died in 1986 before playing a single game for the Celtics. Then in the summer of 1993, Reggie Lewis, Boston's leading scorer, died unexpectedly while preparing to play in a pick-up game.

The Celtics now find themselves rebuilding around Croatian power forward Dino Radja, forward Antoine Walker and sharpshooting point guard Dana Barros, who grew up in Boston. With Auerbach calling the shots, Boston won't be down for long.

Dino Radja: Croatia's 6–11 power house.

23

CHARLOTTE HORNETS

The NBA's Buzz

Considered a long shot when the most recent expansion process started, Charlotte put together a solid plan and found itself with one of four new franchises. With smart marketing moves and even brighter player decisions, the Hornets have become one of the most successful young teams in the league. With underrated forward Glen Rice leading the way, no one doubts Charlotte now.

They came out of nowhere in 1988 and the Charlotte Hornets haven't stopped rolling since.

One of two franchises added to the league prior to the 1988–89 season, Charlotte started making all the right moves immediately. On the court, the Hornets moved patiently while building one of the league's best young teams. Off the court, Charlotte became one of the NBA's most popular franchises by combining basketball success with brilliant marketing.

As a result, Charlotte led the league in attendance in four of its first five seasons. The 23,698-seat Charlotte Coliseum is one of the NBA's largest and loudest arenas, its fans packing the "Hive" for virtually every home game since the team arrived.

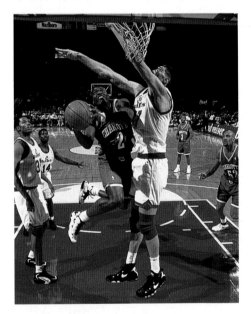

Larry Johnson has taken off for New York.

But there are at least a couple reasons for all the noise and notice. One of those is All-Star forward Larry Johnson. A rugged rebounder and powerful scorer, Johnson became the team's first real pillar. Charlotte used the first pick in the 1991 draft to select Johnson from the University of Nevada-Las Vegas (UNLV). And he didn't disappoint.

Johnson quickly became recognized as one of the best power forwards in the league. He averaged more than 20 points and 10 rebounds in each of his first two seasons. Johnson was named NBA Rookie of the Year in 1992 and a year later was chosen to the All-NBA second team.

"He's a great player," says Detroit Pistons coach Doug Collins. "Larry Johnson isn't afraid to mix it up inside or move outside and take the big shot. He's going to be a star in this league, no question."

But Johnson couldn't get it done alone, and the Hornets struggled through their first four seasons. Then came Alonzo Mourning. Although Orlando's Shaquille O'Neal gained more notoriety during the 1992–93 season, Mourning established himself as one of the best young centers to enter the NBA in years.

The year before Mourning arrived, Charlotte had stumbled to a 31–51 record. Kenny Gattison, though a solid competitor, had been forced to play the middle despite standing just 6–8. Opposing teams

ROLL OF HONOR				
Conference/Division	Eastern/Central			
First NBA year	1988-89			
Home Arena details	Charlotte Coliseum (built 1988, capacity 23,698)			
Former cities/nicknames	None			
NBA Championships	None			
Playing Record	G	W	L	Pct
Regular Season	656	272	384	.415
Playoffs (Series 1-2)	13	5	8	.385

had taken advantage, which forced Johnson to carry much of the offensive and defensive load.

But all that changed with Mourning. The Hornets, under coach Allan Bristow, won 44 regular-season games to make the playoffs for the first time.

Charlotte more than passed its first play-off tests. The Hornets blew by Boston in the First Round of the 1993 postseason and fought the powerful New York Knicks hard before getting eliminated in the Eastern Conference Semifinals.

Injuries to Johnson and Mourning slowed the Hornets' progress after their playoff run in 1993. Johnson came back strong from his injuries in 1995, but Mourning found his days were numbered in a Hornets uniform.

Charlotte traded Mourning to Miami at the start of the 1995–96 season, but the deal netted them another star: Glen Rice, a small forward with seemingly endless three-point range. Rice played in his first All-Star Game after joining the Hornets, helping Charlotte fans to forget the popular Mourning.

Vestiges of Charlotte's embryonic era still remain. Tyrone "Muggsy" Bogues, the league's smallest player at 5–3, and Dell Curry, a long-range shooter, have been with the team since the opening season. Hornets fans had to deal with another blow, however, when Larry Johnson left the Hive to become a Knick. The Hornets will attempt to rebuild around Rice and former Lakers center Vlade Divac.

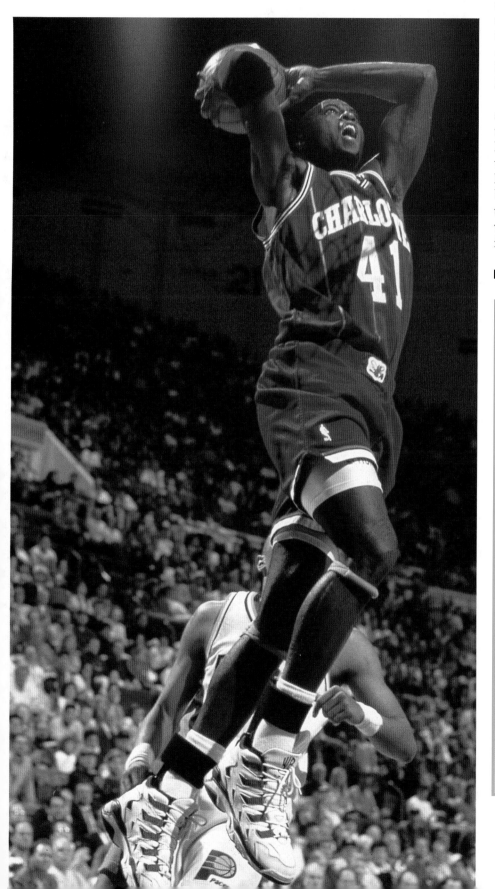

Lift Off: Glen Rice soars through the air.

★ ★ ★ ★ ★ ★ ★ ★ ★ ★ ★

MUGGSY BOGUES
The Sting in the Hornets

Tyrone "Muggsy" Bogues has never thought of himself as small. Although standing just 5–3 and playing a game dominated by giants, he hardly notices.

"They're just taller than me," says Bogues. "That's all."

Even after a solid college career at Wake Forest, few thought Bogues would be able to compete successfully at the NBA level. But the Washington Bullets used the No. 12 pick in the 1987 NBA Draft to select him where he joined the NBA's tallest player, 7–7 Manute Bol.

A year later, Charlotte selected Bogues in the 1988 expansion draft. Within a year, Bogues, despite his size, became a fixture in the Hornets' starting lineup. With incredible quickness and a sixth sense for the ball, Bogues has overcome any problems his size might create.

CHICAGO BULLS

Rebuilding A Winner

With one of the game's greatest players in Michael Jordan, the Chicago Bulls became the first team in more than 25 years to win three straight NBA Championships. Jordan turned a struggling franchise into the dominant team of the early 1990s with a spectacular combination of style and substance that made the Bulls one of the best teams in league history. Following his brief time-out, Air Jordan is back to steer the Bulls to success.

The Chicago Bulls story is a tale of two eras, with defense the single thread connecting them.

When coach Dick Motta took over the Chicago Bulls in 1968, the franchise was was entering its third season. Johnny "Red" Kerr had guided the expansion Bulls into the playoffs in their first two seasons, but management decided it wanted a fresh young coach and hired Motta.

Within a year, Motta had built the offense around a pair of high-scoring forwards in Bob Love and Chet Walker. The defense revolved around Jerry Sloan, whose competitive intensity intimidated many opponents.

From 1970 to 1975, Chicago led the league in defense twice and never finished lower than third. They reached the Western Conference Finals in 1974 and 1975.

Look Up: Toni Kukoc dunks on the Phoenix Suns.

After Motta left in 1976, management acquired aging stars like Artis Gilmore and Larry Kenon. That didn't work, and they compounded the problem with poor draft choices. By 1984 the Bulls needed a savior.

They got three of them.

First, Michael Jordan arrived in the 1984 Draft. Then Jerry Reinsdorf bought the team midway through the 1984–85 season and inserted Jerry Krause as general manager. Krause, who had been a Bulls scout in the late 1960s and early 1970s knew exactly the kind of team he wanted. He had watched Motta win games with defense and like Reinsdorf, who had long admired Red Holzman's New York Knicks, wanted a team that could play both ends of the court.

It took two coaching changes and nearly six seasons, but Krause eventually built a team to complement Jordan's extraordinary talents. The key moves came on a single day in 1987. The Bulls made a deal with Seattle to acquire the draft rights to Scottie Pippen and then selected Horace Grant with their own first-round pick.

A year later the final piece to a championship puzzle arrived in the form of aging 7–1 center Bill Cartwright. Coach Phil Jackson, a player on those Knicks teams that Reinsdorf remembered, built the defense around Jordan, who had become the league's best defensive guard as well as its premier scorer. So it wasn't surprising that the Bulls turned in one of the most dominating playoff performances in history in 1991. Chicago won 15-of-17 playoff games and defeated Magic Johnson's Los Angeles Lakers in the NBA Finals for its first title.

A year later the Bulls won their second straight championship. And then Chicago

ROLL OF HONOR

Conference/Division	Eastern/Central			
First NBA year	1966-67			
Home Arena details	United Center (built 1994, capacity 21,500)			
Former cities/nicknames	None			
NBA Championships	1991, 1992, 1993, 1996			
Playing Record	**G**	**W**	**L**	**Pct**
Regular Season	2459	1316	1143	.535
Playoffs (Series 26-18)	213	117	96	.549

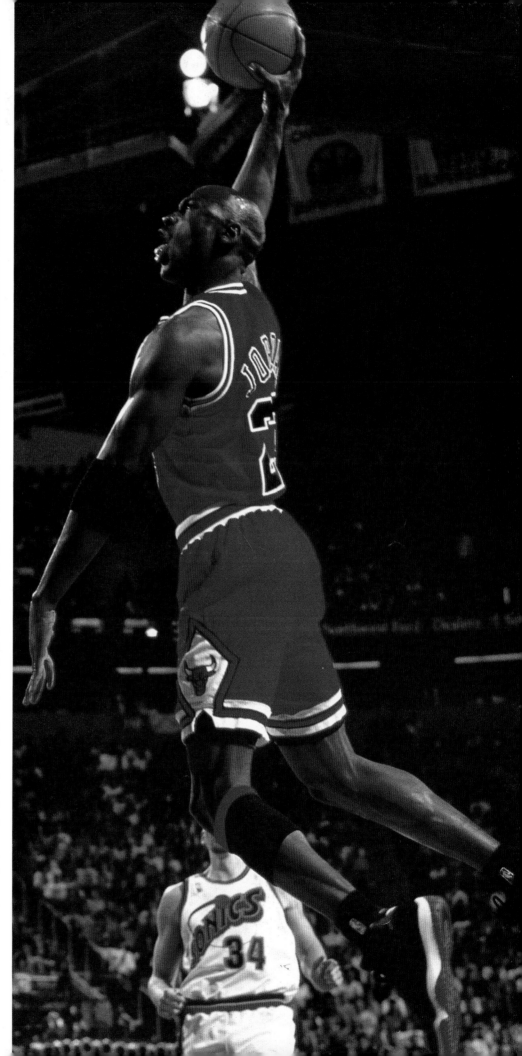

BOB LOVE
A Love Story

That Bob Love, who came from a small Louisiana town with a severe stutter, ever made it in the NBA, much less a record book, is one of the league's great stories of pride and perseverance.

In 1965, Love, a brilliant player at Southern University, wasn't drafted until the fourth round by Cincinnati.

Cut by the Royals, Love ended up in the old Eastern League playing for $50 a game while working part time in a hospital. In 1969, Love joined Chicago.

A year later, Love played all 82 games for the Bulls and led the team in scoring with 21.0 points per game. He went on to lead Chicago in scoring seven straight seasons, never averaging less than 19.1 points a game. Love also made the NBA All-Defensive Second Team three times.

Chicago retired his uniform No. 10 early in the 1993–94 season.

marched back into the Finals for the third consecutive year. Jordan refused to let his team lose. He averaged 41 points in six games against Phoenix, including 55 in Game 4 alone.

In October 1993, Jordan shocked the basketball world with his retirement, and Chicago was unable win a fourth straight title. However, when Jordan returned after a season in minor-league baseball, in March 1995, the glamour returned.

After a disappointing loss to the Magic in the 1995 Eastern Conference Finals, the Bulls stormed back to NBA dominance in 1996. With master rebounder Dennis Rodman aboard, a revitalized Air Jordan led the Bulls to an NBA record 72–10 regular season mark. Chicago cruised through the playoffs with little resistance, defeating the SuperSonics in six games to bring United Center its first NBA title. After a fourth title in six seasons, the Bulls lived up to the statement beneath the statue of Jordan erected outside the United Center: "The best there ever was, the best there ever will be."

Michael Jordan in top form

Back From The Brink

A little more than a decade after nearly collapsing beneath the weight of bad decisions on and off the court, Cleveland has become one of the NBA's most solid franchises. With a revamped front office, committed ownership and coach Mike Fratello, the Cavaliers consistently rank as an Eastern Conference power.

For a while, the Cleveland Cavaliers looked like basketball's version of a roller-coaster. The only problem was no one knew for sure whether the Cavaliers would ever pick up enough steam to climb back up after crashing on the way down.

Like most expansion teams, Cleveland started slowly when it got the green light to take off in 1970. Under coach Bill Fitch, the Cavaliers stumbled early and often. They lost the first 15 games in franchise history before slowly gaining control during their first four seasons.

Players such as Bobby "Bingo" Smith, Walt Wesley and Butch Beard, along with top draft picks Austin Carr, Jim Brewer and Campy Russell, helped fuel a steady climb. After winning 15 games in their first season, the Cavaliers improved to 40 by 1974–75.

And a year later, thanks to a timely trade, the team really started rolling. After a 6–11 start to the 1975–76 season, the Cavaliers traded for aging center Nate Thurmond, a future Hall of Famer. Thurmond's influence helped steady the team, particularly young Jim Chones, and Cleveland began to come together.

The Cavaliers won 43 of their last 65 games to finish 49–33 and charged into the playoffs. Once there, Cleveland dispatched the Washington Bullets in a dramatic seven-game semifinal series. The Cavaliers lost to eventual champion Boston in the Eastern Conference Finals after Chones was sidelined with a broken foot.

It would be the first in a series of bad breaks for Cleveland. Injuries pushed the team on a downhill course that only gathered steam in 1979 when the franchise was sold to Ted Stepien.

Under Stepien's erratic hand, Cleveland went through seven head coaches (including Bill Musselman twice) and never won more than 28 games from 1980 through 1983. Stepien so mismanaged the team that the NBA executive office actually stepped in and awarded the Cavaliers a "bonus" first-round pick in 1983 in an attempt to salvage the franchise.

By then, however, the Cavaliers had bottomed out. When new owners took over in 1983, the only way to go was up and that's exactly where Cleveland headed once Wayne Embry joined the front office and Lenny Wilkens took over as head coach.

Cleveland traded for center Brad Daugherty on Draft Day in 1986 and never looked back. The Cavaliers added All-Stars Mark Price and Larry Nance via trades and bolstered the bench with draft choices such as John "Hot Rod" Williams and Terrell Brandon.

The combination of off-court leadership and on-court talent made Cleveland one of the most successful teams of the late 1980s. Led by Wilkens' even-handed approach, the Cavaliers became one of the Eastern Conference's most dynamic teams.

The offense, keyed by Price and Daugherty, was smooth and efficient. Wilkens, a former All-Star point guard, developed an unselfish approach that made Cleveland among the most difficult teams

ROLL OF HONOR

Conference/Division	Eastern/Central		
First NBA year	1970-71		
Home Arena details	Gund Arena (built 1994, capacity 20,562)		
Former cities/nicknames	None		
NBA Championships	None		

Playing Record	G	W	L	Pct
Regular Season	2132	953	1179	.447
Playoffs (Series 4-12)	73	27	46	.370

in the league to defend. Concentrate too much on Daugherty and Price, one of the NBA's finest outside shooters, would bomb away from the outside.

The Cavaliers appeared on the verge of a championship during the 1988–89 season when they won 57 games and defeated Chicago six times during the regular season.

But the roller coaster ride headed for another set of dips, virtually all of them created by Chicago's Michael Jordan. Jordan's last-second 16-foot jump shot beat Cleveland in the decisive game of the 1989 First-Round Playoff series. Jordan's Bulls struck again in 1992 and once more in 1993, when Jordan's last-second jump shot eliminated Cleveland in the Eastern Conference Semifinals.

Mike Fratello took over as Cavs coach in 1993–94 and revamped the team from top to bottom. Mark Price was traded away, but young players like point guard Terrell Brandon, swingman Bobby Phills and

small forward Chris Mills have stepped to the fore. Small forward Danny Ferry has blossomed into a long-range threat after a lackluster early career, and swingman Dan Majerle was brought in from Phoenix to add toughness and leadership. With Fratello's low-scoring, defensive style, Cleveland remains a tough test for Eastern Conference foes come playoff time.

The Cavaliers were dealt a blow when Daugherty was forced to retire afer the 1995–96 season. Without their big man in the middle, Fratello has been forced to employ a low-scoring, defensive style of play. The Cavs have used this strategy to frustrate more talented opponents and remain a tough test for Eastern Conference foes come playoff time. But until the team replaces Daugherty, Cleveland will be a long shot to win its first NBA title.

Worth the Wait: Terrell Brandon

TERRELL BRANDON
Little Big Man

After being selected in the first round of the 1992 NBA Draft, Terrell Brandon did not immediately become a star—or even a starter, for that matter. After a stellar college career at Oregon, Brandon found himself playing behind Mark Price, Cleveland's long-time starting point guard.

Brandon spent three years in his backup role before injuries to Price earned him a spot in the starting lineup. Unfortunately, Brandon himself fell prey to the injury bug. He suffered through mononucleosis, a stress fracture of the right leg and a sprained wrist, but still impressed the Cavs enough to deal away Price before the 1995–96 season.

Brandon was finally the starting point guard, and he didn't disappoint. He improved his scoring average to 19.3 points (six points per game higher than the previous season) and also registered career highs in assists (6.5) and steals (1.76) in his first full season as a starter. Despite standing less than 6 feet tall, Brandon, who played his first NBA All-Star Game in San Antonio, showed he could play with the big boys. He grabbed 10 rebounds in one game, and blocked 5 shots in another.

Cleveland's small lineup means that Brandon often has to guard much taller players, but he makes up for the disadvantage with court smarts and outstanding skills. If Cleveland add some quality big men to its lineup, look for Brandon to lead them to the top.

The Long Road Back

For years the Dallas Mavericks were recognized as one of the most successful expansion franchises in league history. Building with young talent, the team charged to the top of the Western Conference before age and disappointing personnel moves led to yet another building program. Dallas has reloaded with new young stars and is ready to return to prominence.

For eight years, the Dallas Mavericks pushed all the right buttons and make all the right calls. From their first season in 1980–81, when Coach Dick Motta, long one of the league's master tacticians, poked and prodded a rag-tag expansion roster to 15 victories, the Mavericks defied the gloomiest of expectations.

They improved quickly, winning 43 games in just their fourth season. Three years later, with Motta still at the controls and the roster loaded with talent, Dallas had arrived. The Mavericks took Magic Johnson's Los Angeles Lakers to the seventh game of the Western Conference Finals in 1988. The rise was so rapid and so perfectly executed that Dallas was considered one of the finest organizations in all of professional sports.

Indeed, representatives from Minnesota, Miami, Charlotte and Orlando queried Mavericks' executives prior to joining the league in the NBA's last expansion. How, they all wondered, could a team without a single star player rise to within a single game of the NBA Finals in just seven seasons?

Thanks to a tight-knit front office, a solid coaching staff and enlightened player selection, It started with the team's first NBA Draft in 1981 which produced Mark Aguirre, Rolando Blackman and Jay Vincent. Aguirre and Blackman eventually became two of the league's finest scorers, Aguirre the versatile small forward

Mash Dash: Mashburn goes to the hole.

capable of scoring from anywhere on the court and Blackman the true shooting guard with deadly accuracy.

The 1984 Draft produced Sam Perkins, a versatile 6–11 forward who added yet another scorer and inside defense. Detlef Schrempf arrived in the 1985 Draft with towering 7–2 center James Donaldson coming aboard in a trade. The roster appeared virtually complete when the 1986 Draft produced Roy Tarpley, a multi-talented 6–11 forward.

Tarpley, as it turned out, would provide nearly as many negatives as positives. After

JAMAL MASHBURN
The Cornerstone

The Dallas Mavericks had suffered through one of the worst seasons in NBA history. But as they looked toward the 1993 Draft, even the most pessimistic fan could see a ray of hope.

With the No. 4 pick overall, the Mavericks selected one of the best all-around players in the college ranks. In Jamal Mashburn, from the University of Kentucky, Dallas executives found more than a solid player to lift a sagging franchise. Mashburn developed into a multi-dimensional force. He could block shots, run the floor, pass and score from virtually anywhere on the court.

Although Mashburn was only 22 when the 1994–95 season opened, it didn't take the Mavericks long to realize they had hit the jackpot. Mashburn averaged 19.2 points in his first season and was named to the 1994 All-Rookie First Team.

Mashburn averaged 24.1 points in his second season and was nearly on the same score when a left knee injury ended his third season early. Dallas' hopes hinge on his recovery.

ROLL OF HONOR

Conference/Division	Western/Midwest			
First NBA year	1980-81			
Home Arena details	Reunion Arena (built 1980, capacity 17,502)			
Former cities/nicknames	None			
NBA Championships	None			
Playing Record	**G**	**W**	**L**	**Pct**
Regular Season	1312	541	771	.412
Playoffs (Series 4-6)	48	21	27	.438

a memorable seven-year rise, the franchise turned on his misfortunes. A severe knee injury to Tarpley started the Mavericks in a slow spin that eventually landed Dallas right back where it started. A series of drug-related problems left Tarpley banished from the league until his reinstatement prior to the 1994–95 season.

Aguirre, who had demanded a trade, was sent to Detroit for Adrian Dantley. Then, in an attempt to find another big man, the Mavericks traded Schrempf to Indiana for Herb Williams, only to see Schrempf become an All-Star. If that wasn't enough, Donaldson suffered a knee injury. The team had dropped hard back to the NBA basement.

The team again retooled itself, adding "The Three J's": shooting guard Jimmy Jackson, forward Jamal Mashburn and point guard Jason Kidd. Jackson reminds some of a young Michael Jordan with his complete game and explosive scoring ability. Mashburn is a threat down low or on the perimeter, and Kidd—the 1995 NBA co-Rookie of the Year with Grant Hill—is perhaps the best point guard to enter the NBA since Magic Johnson. Injuries to Mashburn and Jackson have kept the Mavs from reaching their full potential, but former Bulls assistant Jim Cleamons, Dallas' new coach, inherits a roster filled with exciting potential.

Double J in Big D: Jimmy Jackson's explosive offense and all-around play has made him a key to the Dallas future.

Hidden Rocky Mountain Highs

The Denver Nuggets' success in the old ABA had started to fizzle by the time they joined the NBA in 1976. Even the franchise's high scoring teams under Coach Doug Moe came during a decade dominated by Magic Johnson's Los Angeles Lakers. That could change soon, however, as Denver has once more started building a contender with young stars like LaPhonso Ellis and Antonio McDyess.

For all the flash and dash, the golden years have often come at the wrong time for the Denver Nuggets.

When Coach Larry Brown and high-flying superstar David Thompson were crafting 60-win seasons in the mid 1970s, the Nuggets were one of the most exciting shows in the American Basketball Association. Though the team remained strong after merging with the NBA prior to the 1976–77 season, the next surge didn't come until Doug Moe brought his version of run-and-gun basketball to Denver.

The Nuggets reached the playoffs for nine straight seasons under Moe, but always found one Western Conference team too good for them.

Still, the Nuggets have rarely not shined. As one of the 11 charter members of the ABA in 1967, Denver was recognized as one of that league's best run organizations. Originally called the Rockets, Denver stunned the basketball world in 1969 by signing college undergraduate Spencer Haywood.

Haywood, star of the U.S. men's gold medal team at the 1968 Mexico City Olympics, played only one season for Denver. But his signing put the franchise on the professional basketball map while also leading to changes in college eligibility rules, many of which are in place today in the NBA.

In 1974, Carl Scheer, an innovative general manager, took over the team and hired Brown as coach. The Nuggets had a new name and a front office full of new faces, but they became instant contenders on the court.

After winning 65 games during the 1974–75 season, Denver loaded up for an ABA title run. Thompson became the first No. 1 NBA draft pick to sign with the ABA. The same season, Denver landed another rookie, Marvin Webster, and veteran Dan Issel. With Thompson and Issel leading the way, Denver went to the ABA championship series before losing to the New Jersey Nets.

It turned out to be the ABA's finale and Denver's only clear shot at a championship. Ensconced in the NBA's reconfigured Midwest Division, the Nuggets continued a franchise tradition of playoff futility. After winning 50 games in its NBA debut in 1976–77, Denver ran into the championship-bound Portland Trail Blazers in the Conference Semifinals. A year later, Seattle eliminated the Nuggets in the Western Conference Finals.

And despite continued regular-season success under Moe, the Nuggets never reached the NBA Finals. Still, Denver remained one of the greatest scoring shows in league history. During Moe's nine seasons, Denver led the league in scoring five times and never finished out of the top five.

Players like Thompson, Issel, Alex English, Kiki Vandeweghe, George McGinnis and Lafayette "Fat" Lever fueled a relentless offensive attack that

★ ★ ★ ★ ★ ★ ★ ★ ★ ★

LaPHONSO ELLIS
The Patrol Man

Growing up on the tough streets of East St. Louis, Ill., LaPhonso Ellis had a dream to grow up and work in a uniform. Not an NBA uniform, but a policeman's uniform. He would watch the endless patrol cars driving through his neighborhood and imagine himself inside.

"I can't remember any of the other kids feeling that way," says Ellis, a 6–8 power forward. "I think that was highly unusual. But those officers were positive role models for me. You couldn't tell me anything negative about police officers."

The discipline that Ellis taught himself in those early years has carried over to his basketball career. Despite major surgery to both kneecaps that caused him to miss the better parts of two seasons in the NBA, Ellis maintained his desire to play for the Nuggets. When he returned in late 1996, it was as if he hadn't missed a beat.

Instead of patrolling the streets of East St. Louis, Ellis patrols the inside of McNichols Arena. Nuggets fans couldn't be happier.

didn't run out of steam until Moe left following the 1989–90 season.

With Issel as the team's coach, the Nuggets pulled off one of the most dramatic upsets in NBA history by knocking off the heavily favored Seattle SuperSonics in the 1994 NBA Playoffs. With Issel at the helm and young players such as center Dikembe Mutombo, point guard Mahmoud Abdul-Rauf, small forward Rodney Rogers and power forward LaPhonso Ellis, the Nuggets looked like a contender in the making.

But injuries forced Ellis to miss nearly two seasons and Issel stepped down as Denver's coach in 1995. The team has chosen to reshuffle its deck, trading away players like Abdul-Rauf and Rogers for established players like point guard Mark Jackson and shooting guard Sarunas Marciulionis.

The Nuggets also suffered a severe blow when Mutombo took his intimidating presence to the Atlanta Hawks as a free agent. Without Mutombo, the interior shot-blocking duties will fall upon the broad shoulders of power forward Antonio McDyess.

Denver fans find themselves with a team substantially different from that 1994 Cinderella squad that shocked the Sonics. Their fortunes may be uncertain, but any team would be happy to have a healthy Ellis and McDyess patrolling the paint. With Jackson bring the ball up and Marciulionis slashing in from the wing, the Nuggets could be golden again.

Dikembe Mutombe has taken his talents east to play in Atlanta.

ROLL OF HONOR

Conference/Division	Western/Midwest
First NBA year	1976-77
Home Arena details	McNichols Sports Arena (built 1975, capacity 17,022)
Former cities/nicknames	Denver Rockets (1967-74)
NBA Championships	None

Playing Record	G	W	L	Pct
NBA Regular Season	1640	816	824	.498
Combined NBA/ABA	2384	1229	1155	.516
Playoffs (Series 7-14)	98	39	59	.398
Combined NBA/ABA	160	66	94	.413

Witness for the Defense

They didn't win many friends, but the Detroit Pistons certainly influenced opponents. The Pistons turned to defense in the late 1980s and put on a clinic. With a tough, no-nonsense approach, Detroit became one of the greatest defensive teams in the history of the league. The Pistons won a pair of NBA Championships during a five-year run in which they never finished lower than third in overall team defense. With Joe Dumars as a link between past and present, defense is still the pride of the Pistons.

When Detroit finally won the 1989 NBA title, it ended a 40-year journey that included 21 head coaches, one move and a daunting 15-year stretch without a single winning season. Even after the team moved from Fort Wayne, Indiana, to Detroit for the 1957–58 season, 13 straight losing seasons followed.

The franchise started out as the after-hours avocation of Fort Wayne manufacturer Fred Zollner, who owned a factory that made automobile pistons. Zollner first organized the team in 1937, more than a decade before the NBA started. Throughout the mid 1940s, Zollner's Pistons were one of the top teams in the National Basketball League, winning consecutive titles in 1944–45.

But all that changed when the NBL survivors, including the Pistons, joined the NBA. The Pistons immediately established what would become a long-running reputation as everyone's favorite opponent despite some solid, early talent. Not even players such as George Yardley, Max Zaslofsky, Larry Foust and Andy Phillip could prevent the Pistons from general mediocrity during their first decade in the league.

Under coach Charlie Eckman, a former referee, Fort Wayne reached the NBA Finals in 1955 and 1956, but following the move to Detroit in 1957, a .500 playing record was beyond the Pistons.

The first of two major upturns followed with the arrival of 6–11 giant Bob Lanier, Detroit's No. 1 pick in the 1970 Draft. Three years later, the Pistons finished 52–30, their best record to that point, but fell to the Chicago Bulls in the Western Conference Semifinals.

By 1979 Lanier and long-time backcourt star Dave Bing had been traded and the Pistons were again one of the league's

BILL LAIMBEER
No Apologies

Bill Laimbeer will no doubt be remembered for all the wrong things. By the time he retired in 1993, Laimbeer had been one of the most heavily fined players in NBA history.

But Laimbeer also played with an iron spirit that carried him through a 14-year career. Upon leaving Notre Dame Laimbeer spent one season in Europe before signing with Cleveland in 1981. Two years later he landed in Detroit and became an instant contributor.

During Laimbeer's first nine years with the Pistons, he was the team's starting center in 736 of 738 regular season games and never missed a playoff game. He also became a key component in the team's back-to-back championships in 1989 and 1990.

Laimbeer, who had his No. 40 jersey retired by the Pistons in 1995, is Detroit's all-time leader in rebounds and games played, missing just nine games in his 13 full seasons.

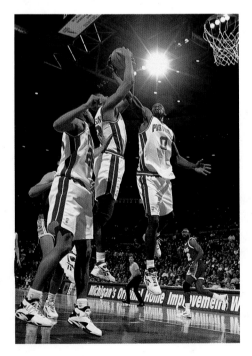

Allan Houston is now scoring for the Knicks.

who would become one of the most accomplished point guards in NBA history. Joe Dumars arrived in the 1985 Draft followed by Dennis Rodman and John Salley in 1986. Trades produced Bill Laimbeer, Vinny Johnson, Mark Aguirre and James Edwards.

Coach Chuck Daly then molded the team into a bruising defensive squad built on strength and toughness. They pushed, shoved, scratched and clawed their way to consecutive championships, winning their first in 1989 by sweeping the Los Angeles Lakers and Magic Johnson 4–0 in the best-of-7 NBA Finals, then adding a second title in 1990 by downing Portland, 4–1.

Daly departed after the 1992 season, and the only member of the Pistons' championship nucleus to remain in the Motor City is Dumars. The highly respected shooting guard is now the elder statesman on a young team with a once-again bright future.

Former Bulls coach Doug Collins is now calling the shots in Detroit, while Grant Hill has become the Pistons' resident superstar. Hill's versatility and explosiveness are complemented by the leadership of Dumars and power forward Otis Thorpe, a veteran of a championship team in Houston. Hill has become air apparent to Michael Jordan as an NBA fan favorite, leading the NBA in All-Star voting in each of his two seasons. To achieve Jordan's illustrious status, he must lead the Pistons past the Bulls and to an NBA Championship.

Hill the Thrill: Grant Hill is one of the game's most popular players.

worst teams. But out of the ashes of a 16–66 1979–80 season rose a Detroit team that would come to dominate the late 1980s.

The Pistons used their No. 1 pick in the 1981 Draft to select Thomas,

ROLL OF HONOR

Conference/Division	Eastern/Central			
First NBA year	1948-49			
Home Arena details	The Palace of Auburn Hills (built 1988, capacity 21,454)			
Former cities/nicknames	Fort Wayne Pistons (1948-57)			
NBA Championships	1989, 1990			
Playing Record	G	W	L	Pct
Regular Season	3776	1783	1993	.472
Playoffs (Series 23-26)	219	111	108	.507

35

Back to the Drawing Board

Before coach Don Nelson took over at Golden State, the Warriors were suffering through the worst period of their existence. But Nelson brought new life to the once proud franchise with a wide-open offense that more than made up for the lack of a big-time center. But in 1995, a combination of injuries, trades and Nelson's sudden resignation found the Warriors trying to map out a new future, behind No. 1 pick Joe Smith.

Another rise has led to another brief fall and Golden State once again is headed back to the future.

The Philadelphia Warriors began play in 1946 as charter members of the 11-team Basketball Association of America. Under the leadership of local basketball legend Eddie Gottlieb and with players such as Joe Fulks, Howard Dallmar and George Senesky, the Warriors won the first BAA title.

It took nine years for the Warriors to capture another championship, this one in the reconfigured NBA. With Senesky as coach, legendary players such as Paul Arizin and Neil Johnston led Philadelphia to a 45–27 regular-season record and an easy rout of the Fort Wayne Pistons in the 1956 Finals.

In 1959, Gottlieb convinced his fellow owners to allow Philadelphia a non-traditional "territorial" draft pick. In that era, each NBA team was allowed to choose one college player from the geographic area of the team's dominant fan base. Gottlieb's coup was predicated on the fact that Wilt Chamberlain had played high school ball in Philadelphia, although he was attending college at the University of Kansas.

Wilt 'The Stilt' would become the greatest scoring machine in NBA history. He stood 7–1, weighed 275 pounds, and immediately became the most dominant individual player the league had ever known. He averaged a phenomenal 50.4 points a game during the 1961–62 season for Philadelphia.

But not even Chamberlain could carry an entire franchise by himself. With attendance lagging, Gottlieb sold the team to a San Francisco group that moved the Warriors west for the 1962–63 season.

Two years later, the Warriors were once again building for a championship run. Nate Thurmond, who would become another of the great NBA centers, arrived. San Francisco then dealt Chamberlain to the new Philadelphia franchise. Thurmond was soon surrounded by players such as Rick Barry, Jeff Mullins, Al Attles and Clyde Lee. And in 1967, the Warriors found themselves back in the NBA Finals, this time against Chamberlain's Philadelphia 76ers, who took the championship 4–2.

It took another 10-year cycle before Golden State reached the Finals again. With Attles now coaching and Barry leading the team in scoring, Golden State, which moved to Oakland from San Francisco prior to the 1971–72 season, swept the Washington Bullets 4–0 for the 1975 NBA Championship.

As before, however, another downturn started gradually over the next decade. It wasn't until another new ownership group hired Coach Don Nelson that the franchise took off again. Nelson brought the Warriors back to life.

With young, talented players such as Chris Mullin, Tim Hardaway, Sarunas Marciulionis and Billy Owens, the Warriors combined to win 55 games during the

1991–92 regular season.

Three years later, fresh off a Draft-day trade that produced a potential superstar in Chris Webber, the Warriors appeared primed for another run at the title. Latrell Sprewell, a gifted and versatile guard, had been added to an arsenal built around

ABOVE Joe Smith has an ordinary name and an extraordinary game.

ROLL OF HONOR

Conference/Division	Western/Pacific		
First NBA year	1946-47		
Home Arena details	Oakland Coliseum Arena (built 1966, capacity 15,025)		
Former cities/nicknames	Philadelphia Warriors (1946-62), San Francisco Warriors (1962-71)		
NBA Championships	1947, 1956, 1975		

Playing Record	G	W	L	Pct
Regular Season	3882	1878	2004	.484
Playoffs (Series 22-24)	214	99	115	.463

Chris Mullin shows why he is one of the NBA's purest shooters.

Mullin and Hardaway to make the Warriors virtually impossible to stop.

Mullin, one of the NBA's greatest shooters, opened to the floor Sprewell and Hardaway. And for the 1994–95 season,

CHRIS MULLIN
A Shooting Star

Chris Mullin started hearing the criticisms in grade school. Some said he was too slow. Others claimed Mullin couldn't jump. And still others wondered if he was quick enough to become a productive player.

They were all wrong. By the time Mullin took his brilliant jump shot from St. John's University to the NBA as Golden State's first-round pick in 1985, he had learned to cover all he lacked in physical talent with an almost fundamentally perfect game.

A five-time All-Star, Mullin took a career scoring average of 21.9 into the 1994–95 season. It was Mullin, along with Michael Jordan and Patrick Ewing, who made the 1984 U.S. men's Olympic basketball team one of the country's greatest. Mullin then won a second Olympic gold medal as a member of the 1992 "Dream Team."

"When God made basketball," said Magic Johnson, "he just carved Chris Mullin out and said, 'This is a basketball player.'"

Golden State added former Miami center Rony Seikaly. With Webber and Seikaly up front, the Warriors appeared to have plugged the team's only remaining holes.

But all the hope dissolved amid injuries to Hardaway and Mullin and a conflict between Nelson and Webber. Golden State eventually traded Webber to Washington for Tom Gugliotta and three future first-round draft picks. Everything became even more clouded as the season dragged on. More injuries to Mullin, Seikaly and Hardaway compounded the problems created by Webber's departure. Gugliotta was quickly traded to Minnesota for forward Donyell Marshall and Nelson resigned.

Though building blocks remained in Mullin, Hardaway, Seikaly and Sprewell, the Warriors were left searching for another architect. And they found two in Coach Rick Adelman and GM Dave Twardzik. As head coach at Portland, Adelman twice took the Trail Blazers to the NBA Finals while Twardzik, who once played for Portland, helped build the Charlotte Hornets into of the Eastern Conference's best teams.

The popular Hardaway was traded away in 1996, but power forward Joe Smith is the newest piece in the Warriors' puzzle. Smith averaged 15.3 points and 8.7 rebounds as a rookie. With the reliable veteran guard B.J. Armstrong on board to assist Smith, Sprewell and Mullin, the future looks Golden again for the Warriors.

The Dream Is Real

Houston used an enormous front line to reach the 1986 NBA Finals. But after Larry Bird's Boston Celtics ended those title dreams, the Rockets took nearly a decade to find a way back. With former star Rudy Tomjanovich coaching and superstar Hakeem "The Dream" Olajuwon doing just about everything else, Houston knocked off New York in a thrilling Game 7 to claim its first championship in 1994 and swept Orlando to repeat in 1995.

Until their dramatic victory in the 1994 NBA Finals, one question had dogged Houston for nearly 20 years. How could any team have had players such as Elvin Hayes, Moses Malone, Ralph Sampson and Hakeem Olajuwon, all as rookies, and reach the early 1990s without a single NBA championship?

The San Diego Rockets joined the league in 1967. As with most expansion teams, the first season was a long one. The immediate result, however, was that San Diego had the No. 1 pick in the 1968 Draft which produced the multi-talented Hayes. Though Hayes led the league in scoring his first season, teams started double and tripling-teaming the 6–9 forward. Opposing teams decided to let the other Rockets beat them, which rarely happened. By 1971, the Rockets were still a sub .500 team and

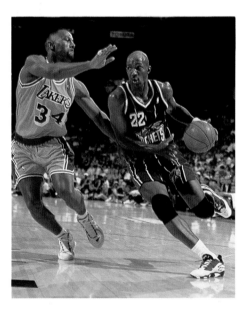

Clyde Drexler storms down the court.

attendance had fallen off in San Diego.

A move to Houston followed, but so too did the losses. A feud between new coach Tex Winter and Hayes led to Hayes being traded in 1972. Despite the presence of young stars like Calvin Murphy and Rudy Tomjanovich, the Rockets needed four years to recover from the Hayes trade. It wasn't until rookie John Lucas and Moses Malone arrived in 1976 that the franchise moved over the .500 mark for the first time. Malone helped lead Houston to 49 victories and the Central Division title.

But once again, the future wasn't nearly as bright as expected. And this time a near tragedy played a part. On Dec. 9, 1977 in a game at Los Angeles, a fight broke out between the Rockets and Lakers. Tomjanovich, trying to be a peacemaker, ran into a punch thrown by Kermit Washington. Tomjanovich ended up in critical condition with terrible facial injuries. Though he eventually recovered, the team limped to 54 losses.

In 1981, with Malone and Murphy leading the way, the Rockets upset Magic Johnson's Los Angeles Lakers in the First Round of the Playoffs. Then they dispatched Midwest Division champion San Antonio and rival Kansas City before losing to Boston in the Finals.

Once more success was fleeting. Within two years, the Rockets were the worst team in basketball. Malone signed with Philadelphia and Houston found itself looking for another great, young center.

ROLL OF HONOR

Conference/Division	Western/Midwest
First NBA year	1967-68
Home Arena details	The Summit (built 1975, capacity 16,279)
Former cities/nicknames	San Diego Rockets (1967-71)
NBA Championships	1994, 1995

Playing Record	G	W	L	Pct
Regular Season	2378	1168	1210	.491
Playoffs (Series 20-16)	174	88	86	.506

Thanks to the NBA Draft, the Rockets found two of them. They drafted 7-4 Ralph Sampson with the No. 1 pick in 1983 and then Hakeem Olajuwon with the first pick in 1984, that duo combined with young Rodney McCray to create one of the most imposing frontlines of that era. Houston reached the 1986 NBA Finals and fought the Boston Celtics valiantly before losing in six games.

Although Sampson was traded in 1989, the Rockets remained dangerous thanks to Olajuwon, but the team didn't come together completely until Tomjanovich took over as head coach in 1992. With Olajuwon, Otis Thorpe, Vernon Maxwell and Kenny Smith leading the way, Houston reached the 1993 Western Conference Semifinals.

It was only the beginning. A year later, the same nucleus carried Houston to victory over Patrick Ewing's New York Knicks in Game 7 of the 1994 Finals, giving Houston

its first NBA Championship.

In 1995, the defending champion Rockets became the first-ever sixth seed to win the title, sweeping Orlando in the Finals, and the fourth consecutive repeat NBA Champion. Houston also set a record by winning seven straight playoff games on the road.

The 1995–96 season saw an unprecedented number of injuries hit the Rockets. Every important member of the team was sidelined, with major injuries to shooting

guard Clyde Drexler and forward Mario Elie. The Rockets made due during the regular season with a makeshift lineup, but they couldn't put together an extended playoff run.

With the nucleus intact from their consecutive championships — and with young players like small forward Robert Horry and point guard Sam Cassell growing into key roles — the Rockets remain a threat to win a third title.

· ·

Hakeem "The Dream" Olajuwon can be a nightmare for opponents.

★ ★ ★ ★ ★ ★ ★ ★ ★ ★ ★ ★ ★

RUDY TOMJANOVICH
Blast from the Past

Midway through the 1991–92 season the Houston Rockets were out of experiments. They had tried virtually everything in search of an elusive NBA Championship.

With the team stuck with a 26–26 record, the franchise finally decided to try one of its own. Rudy Tomjanovich had been a member of the organization since 1970 when he joined the Rockets out of the University of Michigan.

By the time Houston named Tomjanovich interim head coach, he had been involved in the franchise's only two division championships and ranked third on the team's all-time scoring list. The team finished 16–14 under Tomjanovich.

The Rockets had found the man they needed. Houston finished 55–27 in 1992–93 to win the Midwest Division and Tomjanovich was named IBM NBA Coach of the Year. He topped that feat by coaching Houston to back-to-back NBA Championships in 1994 and 1995.

Picking Up The Pace

Pacers®

The Indiana Pacers have one of the more storied histories in all of basketball, but virtually all of it occurred before the team joined the NBA in 1976. As a charter member of the American Basketball Association, Indiana had some of the most dominant teams in that league's brief history. Since joining the NBA, however, the Pacers have worked hard to reclaim their past success.

Despite being situated in a state known for its wildly devoted basketball fans, the Indiana Pacers have spent much of their NBA existence trying to develop a following.

High school basketball has its roots in the small towns of Indiana, while Indiana University has one of the most visible programs in the country. So when the Pacers entered the old ABA as a charter member in 1967, they had much to prove.

They never blinked.

With early stars like Mel Daniels, Roger Brown and Freddie Lewis, Indiana won 59 games and the ABA championship in 1970. One year later, the Pacers stepped on the toes of neighboring Indiana University

Gentle Giant: 7–4 Rik Smits controls the middle.

by signing undergraduate George McGinnis, a brilliant young forward.

McGinnis paid off immediately. He led the Pacers to consecutive ABA titles. Under the leadership of Coach Bobby "Slick" Leonard, the Pacers were a hit on and off the court. Indiana was one of the four surviving ABA franchises to join the NBA in 1976.

But that signaled the end of an era for the Pacers. Leonard was faced with a massive rebuilding job after McGinnis signed with the Philadelphia 76ers in 1975 and age caught up with the rest of the ABA cast.

Selfless Don Buse and high-scoring Billy Knight were the Pacers' early NBA stars,

ROLL OF HONOR

Conference/Division	Eastern/Central
First NBA year	1976-77 (ABA 1967-76)
Home Arena details	Market Square Arena (built 1974, capacity 16,530)
Former cities/nicknames	None
NBA Championships	None (ABA – 1970, 1972, 1973)

Playing Record	G	W	L	Pct
NBA Regular Season	1640	737	903	.449
Combined NBA/ABA	2384	1164	1220	.488
Playoffs (Series 4-8)	59	26	33	.441
Combined NBA/ABA	178	95	83	.534

but the franchise never quite got rolling. The team's first NBA Playoff series didn't come until 1981, a 3-game sweep by Philadelphia, led by ex-Pacer McGinnis, and the Pacers didn't *win* a playoff game until 1987. Along the way there were seven coaches and a four-year period in the early 1980s when Indiana averaged 58 losses per season.

The Pacers, however, were not without some individual gems even during the most difficult times. Players such as Detlef Schrempf, Clark Kellogg, Steve Stipanovich, Herb Williams, Chuck Person, Wayman Tisdale and others, have passed through the franchise.

The team, coached by the legendary Jack Ramsay, finished 41–41 and reached the Playoffs in 1987. Indiana not only earned its first playoff victory, but it appeared to have finally turned itself around.

But Kellogg, who had suffered a severe knee injury four games into the 1986–87 season, never returned. A year later, Stipanovich, a 7-foot center who had developed into a solid player, suffered a career-ending injury. Suddenly, the Pacers were losing games in bunches once more.

Another injection of young talent helped bring Indiana back into the playoff picture. Reggie Miller, one of the league's finest shooters, and 7–4 center Rik Smits helped the Pacers into the playoffs six straight seasons through the 1994–95 campaign.

With coach Larry Brown assuming control of the team and Derrick McKey arriving in a trade for Schrempf, the Pacers finally broke out in 1994. After a franchise-best 47 regular season victories, Indiana rode Miller's brilliant shooting to the Eastern Conference Finals where the Pacers lost a dramatic Game 7 in New York, and in 1995 they lost again in the seventh game of the Eastern Conference

Finals, this time to Orlando.

An untimely injury to Miller kept the Pacers from making an impact on the Eastern Conference playoff picture in 1996. But the addition of young point guard Jalen Rose — at 6–8 a Magic Johnson prototype — has the Pacers ready for a run at the NBA Finals.

Miller Time: Perhaps the NBA's greatest all-around shooter, Reggie Miller takes off for the basket and another two points.

RIK SMITS
Indiana's Gentle Giant

Long before Rik Smits crossed the Atlantic Ocean on his way to an NBA career, he could be found on basketball courts in Eindhoven, Holland. Though blessed with unusual size, (he stands 7–4), and excellent coordination, Smits hadn't had the typical early training of American players by the time he left Holland for the relative obscurity of tiny Marist College in New York.

But the Indiana Pacers took notice and were so impressed they made him the second overall pick in the 1988 NBA Draft. Smits has occupied the middle of the Indiana offense and defense ever since. His soft shooting touch has helped open Indiana's outside game for teammates like Reggie Miller.

Smits scored a career-best 17.9 points per game while shooting 52.6 percent from the floor in 1995. And as the Pacers won their first Central Division title in 1995, Smits was a key part of the team's rise.

LOS ANGELES CLIPPERS

Still Striving For Success

No franchise has tried harder or struggled longer than the Los Angeles Clippers. Originally known as the Buffalo Braves, the team moved to San Diego and then Los Angeles. Once there the franchise was overshadowed by the brilliant Los Angeles Lakers teams led by Magic Johnson. For 12 straight seasons in the late 1970s and 1980s, the Clippers failed to register a winning season. Though the Clippers rose briefly in the early 1990s, the struggle hasn't ended yet.

When the Los Angeles Clippers moved from San Diego in 1984, some worried about the franchise having an identity crisis. After all, one of the league's most successful franchises, the Lakers, had long been a resident of Los Angeles.

Indeed, no team has suffered as much or as long as the Clippers in what seems to be a never-ending quest for respectability.

Since they entered the league as the Buffalo Braves in 1970, the Los Angeles Clippers have won more than half their games just five times. They went 15 straight seasons without a playoff appearance from 1976 through 1991.

To make matters worse, the Clippers have had nine different coaches in 11 years, the latest being Bill Fitch who took over prior to the 1994–95 campaign.

The franchise started its long climb as one of three expansion teams, along with Cleveland and Portland, added for the 1970–71 season. Thanks to wise drafting and the addition of Coach Jack Ramsay, Buffalo had a flashy young lineup loaded with potential by its fourth NBA season.

High scoring center/forward Bob McAdoo along with Randy Smith, Ernie DiGregorio, Jim McMillan, Garfield Heard and veteran Jack Marin, led Buffalo into the playoffs in 1974. McAdoo led the

Lamond Murray rises above the nets.

league in scoring, averaging more than 30 points a game, and Buffalo was the NBA's best offensive team.

The team won 49 games the following season and then 46, each followed by strong, yet limited playoff performances. But the future disintegrated just as it appeared to be taking shape.

Ramsay resigned to take over in Portland. McMillan and DiGregorio were traded and, in a move that disillusioned

ROLL OF HONOR

Conference/Division	Western/Pacific
First NBA year	1970-71
Home Arena details	LA Memorial Sports Arena (built 1959, capacity 16,005)
Former cities/nicknames	Buffalo Braves (1970-78), San Diego Clippers (1978-84)
NBA Championships	None

Playing Record	G	W	L	Pct
Regular Season	2132	778	1354	.365
Playoffs (Series 1-5)	32	13	19	.406

Buffalo fans, McAdoo was dealt along with future United States Congressman Tom McMillen to the New York Knicks for cash and journeyman center John Gianelli.

The moves, coupled with disappointing results on the court, led to poor attendance and the franchise's eventual relocation to San Diego. With Coach Gene Shue now in charge, the Clippers posted a 43–39 record in 1978–79, their last winning mark for more than a decade.

Once again, a disastrous off-season trade had undermined the franchise. This time Kermit Washington, Kevin Kunnert, a first-round pick and cash were shipped to Portland for the remarkable, but often injured Bill Walton. Unfortunately, however, the trade only made things more difficult. Walton, a wondrously talented center, played just 14 games over the next three seasons and the Clippers went into a tailspin.

Although poor seasons translated into great draft positions, the Clippers failed to benefit. From 1987 through 1989, the team used six first-round picks on Reggie Williams, Joe Wolf, Ken Norman, Danny Manning, Hersey Hawkins and Danny

Ferry, none of whom were with the team when the 1994–95 season started.

The Clippers finally found a measure of success when Larry Brown took over as coach midway through the 1991–92 season. They finished 23–12 over their last 35 games and made the playoffs for the first time since 1976. The team made a return trip in 1993 before problems surfaced again.

Not only did Brown leave for Indiana, but Norman, Ron Harper and Dominique Wilkins, who had been acquired in a deal for Manning, departed via free agency.

For the Clippers, the struggle has become more difficult. The team, led by Loy Vaught and Lamond Murray, as well as newcomers Rodney Rogers and swingman Brent Barry—the 1996 NBA Slam-Dunk Champion—the challenge of becoming a consistent playoff contender remains.

Loy Vaught (35, right) goes to work on Portland Trail Blazer forward Cliff Robinson.

LOY VAUGHT
Coming on Strong

Loy Vaught had played in the shadows so long that not even he knew what would happen when he emerged.

At the University of Michigan, Vaught played with stars like Glen Rice, Gary Grant and Rumeal Robinson. Since Vaught joined the Clippers as a first-round pick in the 1990 NBA Draft, Danny Manning, Ron Harper, Dominique Wilkins and others have all passed through Los Angeles.

But when the 1994–95 season opened, so too did Vaught's opportunity. He was the only regular that had been with the Clippers more than three seasons, during which time Vaught had developed into a solid power forward.

In 1993–94, Vaught improved his field goal percentage for the fourth consecutive season to an impressive .537. He added career bests in rebounds, steals, assists points. And in 1994-95, Vaught stepped up as the Clippers' leading scorer and rebounder at 17.5 ppg and 9.7 rpg.

"I've always been, and I prefer to be, a complementary player," says Vaught. "So this is a little different."

So far, however, the Clippers aren't complaining. For a team in need of a foundation, a 6–9, 240-pound forward with Vaught's work ethic is a nice place to start.

The West's Winningest Team

The names are some of the most famous in all of professional basketball. Players like George Mikan, Jerry West, Elgin Baylor, Wilt Chamberlain, Kareem Abdul-Jabbar and Magic Johnson all played on Lakers teams that won NBA Championships. Now the Lakers have added another big name—Shaquille O'Neal. Forget "Showtime," the Lakers are now "Shaqtime."

The Lakers, who started out in Minneapolis, have won 11 Championships, 24 conference titles and own the second best winning percentage in NBA history (.606 entering the 1994–95 season). Only the Celtics, which had won 63.2 percent of their regular season games entering the 1994–95 season, have won more often.

The team was named after Minnesota's claim as the "Land of 10,000 Lakes." It also earned its first championships there, mainly with George Mikan manning the middle. Mikan, basketball's first dominant big man, stood 6–10 and won three straight scoring titles after the Lakers

Cedric Ceballos: A reserve in Phoenix, a star in L.A.

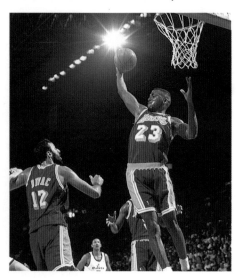

became part of the NBA in 1948.

Mikan played on seven championship teams in his first eight professional season, the first two for Chicago in the old National Basketball League. When that team disbanded, Mikan landed with the Minneapolis franchise in the NBA and helped that team to five titles in six years. Mikan's supporting cast included Slater Martin, Vern Mikkelsen, Jim Pollard and 1952 U.S. Olympic team hero Clyde Lovellette. When Mikan retired after the 1953–54 season, the Lakers last championship, the Lakers needed another star. They found one in 1958 when owner Bob Short signed University of Seattle star Elgin Baylor. Minneapolis reached the NBA Finals in 1959, but was quickly eliminated by Boston and Bill Russell, and the Lakers were off to Los Angeles.

Despite a talented roster that included Baylor and Jerry West, the Lakers kept running into Boston. From 1961 through 1970, Los Angeles won seven Western Division championships. But they lost all seven Finals, six to the Celtics.

Los Angeles' NBA frustrations ended briefly in 1971–72, when an aging Wilt Chamberlain joined the team. In perhaps the greatest single season in NBA history, the Lakers set records with a 33-game winning streak and a 69–13 record.

Though the Lakers reached the Finals the following season, they didn't win another Championship until Johnson

arrived in 1979. The team won a coin flip with the Chicago Bulls for the No. 1 pick in the 1979 Draft and chose Johnson.

JERRY WEST
All-Around Brilliance

Until Michael Jordan teamed with Magic Johnson on the Dream Team, the world had never seen a better backcourt than that of Jerry West and Oscar Robertson during the 1960 Rome Olympics.

In fact, until Jordan, West and Robertson were considered the two greatest shooting guards to ever play the game. Shorter at 6–2 and a more pure shooter and defender, West and the 6–5 Robertson went head-to-head through their entire NBA careers.

Despite leading the Lakers into the NBA Finals nine times, West's only championship came in 1972. But he knew how to win, as evidenced by a career that remains among the most successful in history.

West led the Lakers to the 1977 Pacific Division title in his first year as the team's head coach. Four years later, West moved to the front office and carefully constructed a Lakers team that would dominate the 1980s.

ROLL OF HONOR

Conference/Division	Western/Pacific			
First NBA year	1948-49			
Home Arena details	The Great Western Forum (built 1967, capacity 17,505)			
Former cities/nicknames	Minneapolis Lakers (1948-60)			
NBA Championships	1949, 1950, 1952, 1953, 1954, 1972, 1980, 1982 1985, 1987, 1988			

Playing Record	G	W	L	Pct
Regular Season	3777	2292	1485	.607
Playoffs (Series 73-33)	507	301	206	.594

The 6–9 guard teamed with another legendary big man, Kareem Abdul-Jabbar, and quickly helped the Lakers become the dominant team of the 1980s. The head-to-head matchups with Boston continued, but this time the Lakers came out on top often—winning twice in three NBA Finals meetings.

Los Angeles, with supporting players such as Jamaal Wilkes, James Worthy, Byron Scott, Norm Nixon and Michael Cooper, won five championships in Johnson's first nine seasons.

Johnson and Bird, like Chamberlain and Russell before them, identified an entire decade. Indeed their battles might have been the greatest in league history given their respective skills.

As with Boston, however, those days have given way to another rebuilding process. And that process, at least for the Lakers, appeared to pick up steam during the 1994–95 season. With veteran coach Del Harris taking over the coaching duties, young players Nick Van Exel and Eddie Jones combined with veterans Cedric Ceballos, Vlade Divac and Elden Campbell to give the franchise new life.

Late in the 1995–96 season, the NBA was treated to a comeback from Johnson, who still had the old magic. Playing both power forward and point guard, Magic tried to teach his younger teammates about winning in the playoffs. Yet even Johnson's return failed to rally the Lakers past the Rockets in the first round of the playoffs.

It was hard to top the news of Magic's return, but the Lakers did it when they acquired another bit of Magic—former Orlando center Shaquille O'Neal. While Johnson's future plans are up in the air, the possible pairing of Shaq and Magic is enough to excite any NBA fan.

Nick Van Exel has become one of the league's great young point guards.

Not Standing Pat

With a solid plan and front office patience, the Heat took just four seasons to reach the playoffs after joining the NBA as an expansion franchise in 1988. Miami improved each of its first four seasons in the league before injuries slowed its progress. Now the Heat has gone back to the drawing board in hopes of reclaiming its future. Coach Pat Riley and center Alonzo Mourning are trying to turn the Heat around.

Few NBA expansion franchises have come together with the class and conviction of Miami. While former NBA great Billy Cunningham dreamed of a team in Miami, a city that until 1988 had only one professional sports team in football's Dolphins, critics wondered whether locals would gather regularly to watch basketball, particularly the NBA brand.

But Cunningham persevered. He lined up investors such as Zev Bufman, a highly

He's On Fire: Alonzo Mourning

successful Broadway producer, Ted Arison, owner of the Carnival Cruise Lines, and long-time NBA executive Lewis Schaffel.

With indisputable credentials, Cunningham's group was awarded an NBA franchise in April, 1987. The team quickly became known as the "Heat" and Cunningham and Schaffel went to work on building a roster. A little over a year later, Miami played its first game, joining the expansion Minnesota Timberwolves for the 1988–89 season.

Two of Miami's early building blocks were on the team opening night. Center Rony Seikaly, a first-round pick in the 1988 draft, and Grant Long, a hard-working forward, joined a group of veterans that included Jon Sunvold and Rory Sparrow.

Not surprisingly, the Heat stumbled badly losing its first 17 NBA games and finishing just 15–67. Rookies Glen Rice and Sherman Douglas arrived for the 1989–90 season, but the young Heat continued to stumble and fall, this time to 66 losses.

By the third season, however, Miami had quietly assembled a nucleus of young talent. Though they were still learning on the job—Miami finished 24–58—the future was slowly coming into focus. That's when Cunningham turned to long-time friend and former teammate Kevin Loughery to assume the coaching reins.

Loughery's first team finished 38–44 and became the first of the four newest expansion teams to reach the playoffs. Rookie point

★★★★★★★★★★★★

PAT RILEY
A Winner at Every Stop

Pat Riley has always been a winner. As a reserve guard, Riley won an NBA Championship ring in 1972 with the Lakers. As a Lakers assistant coach, Riley won a second ring in 1980. After taking over as the Lakers' head coach, he would coach Magic Johnson and Kareem Abdul-Jabbar to titles in 1982, '85, '87 and '88. Six NBA Championships. A pretty impressive resumé, to be sure.

In all, Riley has coached his teams to the playoffs in each of his 14 NBA seasons. In fact, Riley's first season in Miami marked the first time one of his teams did not win at least 50 games. After nine years as the Lakers' coach and four seasons at the New York Knicks' helm, Riley has become known for an intense style of defense and for being a master motivator. Perhaps no other coach gets more out of his role players.

Riley has also earned a reputation as one of the most aggressive dealers in the NBA. He acquired Alonzo Mourning at the outset of the 1995–96 season to add a dominant center to the Heat lineup. Miami's 1996 postseason ended quickly, but Riley is preparing the team for long-term success.

guard Steve Smith proved to be even better than advertised while Rice had developed into one of the NBA's finest long-range shooters. Seikaly improved to 16.8 points and 11.8 rebounds a game and Miami appeared to be progressing ahead of even its own long-term schedule.

Then a rash of injuries jolted the franchise during the 1992–93 season. Despite adding flashy rookie Harold Miner and trading for former Detroit Pistons forward John Salley, Miami slipped to a 36–46 record and failed to reach the playoffs. The season, which started with high expectation, faded fast as injuries to Salley, Seikaly, Smith and Willie Burton took their toll. Salley missed 31 games, Smith 34, Burton 56 and Seikaly 10. Only two players on the entire roster appeared in more than 73 of the team's 82 games.

Still, there remained plenty of reason for optimism as Miami made it back to the Playoffs in 1994. Within months, however, a cloud had parked over Miami: Brian Shaw left via free agency; Smith and Long were dealt to Atlanta, Burton to Philadelphia and Seikaly to Golden State; Loughery was replaced by his assistant,

Alvin Gentry, midway through the 1994–95 season, and even the ownership position controlled by Cunningham and Schaffel sold its interest and moved on.

For Miami, the task of rebuilding has been given to former NBA player and coach Dave Wohl, the team's new general manager.

As the team's original ownership moved on, Miami's future was placed in the capable hands of Pat Riley. The former Lakers and Knicks coach didn't waste any time making changes to the Heat. Center Alonzo Mourning, point guard Tim

Hardaway and forward Walt Williams were all added during the 1995–96 season, and the Heat learned to play Riley's stifling brand of defense. Mourning flourished in Miami, becoming the team's leader. With Riley at the helm and the powerful Alonzo Mourning intimidating Heat opponents, Miami fans finally have a reason to cheer.

••••••••••••••••••••••••••••••

Pat Riley: One of the NBA's greatest coaches

R O L L O F H O N O R				
Conference/Division	Eastern/Atlantic			
First NBA year	1988-89			
Home Arena details	Miami Arena (built 1988, capacity 15,200)			
Former cities/nicknames	None			
NBA Championships	None			
Playing Record	**G**	**W**	**L**	**Pct**
Regular Season	656	247	409	.377
Playoffs (Series 0-3)	11	2	9	.182

Rebuilding for The Future

Although the Milwaukee Bucks reached the playoffs for 12 straight seasons from 1980 through 1991, they were never quite good enough to reach the NBA Finals. Now the franchise is working on a new look. The roster is younger, the defense better and the future brighter. All-Star Vin Baker and Glenn Robinson are trying to recapture Milwaukee's past glory.

Few will ever forget the one stroke of luck that turned an expansion franchise into an NBA champion in just three seasons. Basketball history turned on the flip of a single coin in 1969. The Bucks had entered the NBA prior to the 1968–69 season and proceeded to lose 55 games. There were only two divisions in those days, and Phoenix, another expansion team that season, lost 66 games to finish last in the West. Since Milwaukee occupied the bottom spot in the East, a coin flip determined which team would have the No. 1 draft pick in 1969.

No game for either team had been as big as the coin flip. The winner would get 7–2 center Kareem Abdul-Jabbar (then known as Lew Alcindor), at the time the most accomplished center to leave the college ranks since Bill Russell and Wilt Chamberlain. And he didn't disappoint.

Phoenix called heads, the coin came up tails and Milwaukee became an instant contender. Abdul-Jabbar averaged 28.8 points and 14.5 rebounds as a rookie and

the Bucks improved to 55 victories.

Milwaukee then added aging superstar Oscar Robertson prior to the 1970–71 season to run the offense and take pressure off the young Abdul-Jabbar. The Bucks dominated the league, winning 66 games and cruising through the playoffs. They pounded Baltimore in the Finals, winning four straight games by an average of more than 12 points.

Though Abdul-Jabbar led the Bucks to an average of 61 victories over the next three seasons, Milwaukee reached the NBA Finals only once more, in 1974, losing in seven games to Boston.

Injuries plagued Abdul-Jabbar's final season in Milwaukee and the team dipped to 38–44. The Bucks decided to trade Abdul-Jabbar to the Los Angeles Lakers prior to the 1975–76 season. The deal, with journeyman Walt Wesley, produced four young players in return including Elmore Smith, Brian Winters, Dave Meyers and Junior Bridgeman.

But it wasn't until Coach Don Nelson arrived early in the 1976–77 season that the franchise turned around. He built around young players such as Bridgeman, Marques Johnson, Quinn Buckner and Sidney Moncrief. Later, veterans like Bob Lanier helped carry the Bucks through a period of seven straight seasons with 50 or more victories.

Although they continually ran into the Philadelphia 76ers and Boston Celtics in the

ROLL OF HONOR

Conference/Division	Eastern/Central			
First NBA year	1968-69			
Home Arena details	Bradley Center (built 1988, capacity 18,633)			
Former cities/nicknames	None			
NBA Championships	1971			

Playing Record	G	W	L	Pct
Regular Season	2296	1271	1025	.554
Playoffs (Series 16-18)	169	85	84	.503

GLENN ROBINSON
The Bucks' Big Dog

Milwaukee Bucks general manager Mike Dunleavy knew the future had arrived when he used the No. 1 overall pick in the 1994 NBA Draft to select Glenn Robinson.

An unusually intense and gifted small forward, Robinson brought the kind of scoring and rebounding skills Dunleavy's young Bucks had been missing. And Robinson, nicknamed "Big Dog," hasn't disappointed.

The 6–9 forward immediately became Milwaukee's primary scoring threat from anywhere on the court. Not only can he move outside and drain three-pointers, but Robinson is even more dangerous around the basket. Robinson's quickness and leaping ability make him virtually impossible to stop in the paint. All of which helped turn the Bucks into a playoff contender in 1995.

But it's Robinson's work ethic that could turn him into one of the league's brightest stars.

"He works extremely hard," says Dunleavy. "And he's only going to get better."

Despite missing all of training camp, Robinson's often spectacular rookie season landed him on the NBA All-Rookie First Team.

playoffs, Milwaukee remained one of the league's most successful franchises.

In the early 1990s, the team's fortunes took a downturn. The Bucks hit bottom and were forced to rebuild through the NBA Draft. Power forward Vin Baker and small forward Glenn "Big Dog" Robinson were acquired through the Draft, and each had an immediate impact. Baker was an All-Star by 1996, while Robinson was named to the 1996 U.S. Olympic team.

With the considerable offensive talents of Baker and Robinson on the inside and three-point threats like guards Ray Allen—the No. 5 pick in the 1996 NBA Draft who was acquired from Minnesota in a draft-day trade—and Shawn Respert working the outside, the Bucks under new coach Chris Ford, appear ready to return to their earlier form.

LEFT: Glenn Robinson fires off a no-look pass.
RIGHT: Versatile Vin Baker shows his stuff against New York.

Those Howling Wolves

It took 29 years, but Minnesota finally found its way back into the NBA with the Timberwolves. The Minneapolis Lakers won five championships in that city before moving to Los Angeles in 1960. The void was filled when the Timberwolves joined the NBA as an expansion team in 1989. Now all the Timberwolves have to do is win enough to make locals forget about the Lakers.

After five losing seasons, three coaches and several front office changes, the Minnesota Timberwolves are still trying to find their trail to success in the NBA. Minnesota has lost an average of over 60 games a season, hardly the kind of performance Timberwolves fans had expected in a city that produced one of the most successful franchises in NBA history.

In the 1940s and 1950s, Minneapolis was the home of the Lakers. Those Laker teams won five NBA titles in six years before moving to Los Angeles in 1960. So fans in Minneapolis, a group that includes Mikan, met their new team with a clear sense of expectation. Two local businessmen, Harvey Ratner and Marv Wolfenson, were awarded the team in April, 1987.

What followed was a painstaking process of building the ideal franchise. But some

Man with a Mission: Isaiah Rider has only one thing on his mind—scoring points.

early decisions, particularly the hiring of one-time University of Minnesota coach Bill Musselman, backfired. Musselman's teams won games, but he was criticized for failing to develop the young talent and was dismissed. He left in his second season and was replaced by former player Sidney Lowe.

Christian Laettner was drafted in 1992 and the 6–11 forward had an outstanding rookie season, averaging 18.2 points and 8.7 rebounds. Before the 1992–93 season, the team traded for forward Chuck Person and point guard Micheal Williams.

The new Timberwolves were expected to give the team versatility and veteran leadership. But neither Person nor Williams shot very well and Minnesota's slow-paced offense foundered as the team finished last in the league. The 1993–94 season opened with measured optimism with the additions of high-scoring rookie guard Isaiah Rider and Mike Brown, a veteran forward. Bill Blair, a veteran NBA assistant coach, took over the team at the start of the 1994–95 season. In early 1995, the Timberwolves decided to build around Laettner and Rider by trading youth for experience. Rookie Donyell Marshall was dealt to Golden State for veteran Tom Gugliotta. In May 1995, the Timberwolves turned to Minnesota native Kevin McHale to be the architect of their building effort.

McHale made bold moves in attempting to put some teeth into the Wolves' attack. He started by drafting Kevin Garnett, a

ROLL OF HONOR

Conference/Division	Western/Midwest			
First NBA year	1989-90			
Home Arena details	Target Center (built 1990, capacity 19,006)			
Former cities/nicknames	None			
NBA Championships	None			

Playing Record	G	W	L	Pct
Regular Season	574	152	422	.265
Playoffs		Yet to qualify		

★ ★ ★ ★ ★ ★ ★ ★ ★ ★ ★ ★ ★

KEVIN GARNETT
Growing Up in the NBA

After their senior year of high school, most top basketball prospects are deciding which college to attend. Kevin Garnett chose to eliminate that step altogether and start his NBA career at the tender age of 19.

The 6–10, 220-pound power forward became the latest in a short line of NBA players with no college experience. One of the greatest centers in NBA history, Moses Malone, and Seattle power forward Shawn Kemp each became stars without any college experience. However, not every high school phenom who chose the NBA over college was so lucky.

Despite the odds against him, Garnett entered the 1995 NBA Draft after his senior year at Chicago's Farragut Academy. He was chosen fifth overall by the Wolves and became the youngest player in the NBA. Was he ready? Yes.

Garnett struggled briefly as he adjusted to life on the NBA road. Then he proved himself worthy of being in the league. In his first season, Garnett averaged 10.4 points and 6.3 rebounds a game while setting a club record with 131 blocked shots.

"He's got the complete package," says Kevin McHale, the former Celtics great and current Minnesota VP of basketball operations. "He's going to be a force in this league."

power forward who jumped to the NBA after his senior year of high school. He then traded Laettner to Atlanta after the veteran forward and Garnett had a falling out. Garnett's status as the team's leader was cemented when the Wolves acquired point guard Stephon Marbury, the No. 4 selection in the 1996 NBA Draft, in a draft-day swap with Milwaukee. Marbury and Garnett are close friends, and the two will surely have an immediate impact on the court. The explosive scoring of Rider, the potential of Garnett and Marbury, and the leadership of McHale are finally giving the Minnesota faithful a reason to cheer.

• •

New Kid on the Block: Kevin Garnett shows a maturity way beyond his years.

Looking for Respect

The glory years came and went with Julius Erving and the old American Basketball Association. Since entering the NBA in 1976, the Nets have moved from New York to New Jersey, yet they remain overshadowed by the New York Knicks. New coach John Calipari is now charged with forging an identity for the Nets, who feature 7–6 Shawn Bradley.

They played their first games inside a dingy Armory just across the Hudson River from New York City's bright lights. And despite moving all around the New York and New Jersey before finding a lasting home in the Meadowlands, the Nets survived, indeed thrived with a constantly changing roster that at one time or another has included some of the greatest players in basketball history.

The Nets were born out of the ABA's notion that no real sports league could survive without a strong franchise in the New York area. During the 1967–68 season, the Nets had to forfeit one home game because of water on the Armory floor. Another game had to be moved to a high school gym because of scheduling conflicts with a circus.

Within a year, the Nets had moved to Commack Arena on Long Island where they nearly self-destructed. A 17–61 season sent the franchise in a spin that didn't stop until businessman Roy Boe stepped in and bought the team. He made three moves that turned the franchise around. Boe signed Coach Lou Carneseca, moved the team to Island Garden Arena, also on Long Island, and traded a first-round draft pick and a bundle of cash to the struggling Virginia franchise for Rick Barry.

Barry, one of the greatest scorers in professional basketball history, became the franchise's first true superstar. Barry led the Nets to the 1972 ABA Finals before near disaster struck again. A federal judge ordered Barry back to his former NBA team, the Golden State Warriors, for whom Barry had originally signed out of college.

After yet another arena move, to the Nassau Coliseum, the Nets found salvation once more in the struggling Squires. One the most lopsided deals in basketball history sent young Julius Erving to the Nets.

With former NBA player Kevin Loughery now coaching the team, Erving led the Nets to two ABA titles and helped put the entire

Shawn Bradley (45) using his impressive stature.

ROLL OF HONOR

Conference/Division	Eastern/Atlantic			
First NBA year	1976-77 (ABA 1967-68)			
Home Arena details	Continental Airlines Arena (built 1981, cap. 20,029)			
Former cities/nicknames	New Jersey Americans (1967-68),			
	New York Nets (1968-77),			
NBA Championships	None (ABA – 1974, 1976)			

Playing Record	G	W	L	Pct
NBA Regular Season	1640	660	980	.402
NBA/ABA combined	2384	1034	1350	.434
Playoffs (Series 1-9)	36	9	27	.250
NBA/ABA combined	105	46	59	.438

league on the basketball map. Indeed, the Nets were one of only four ABA teams to survive and join the NBA.

The franchise, however, would never be the same. A complicated and controversial deal landed Erving in Philadelphia and the Nets back at the drawing board. In 1977, after yet another arena switch, to Piscataway, N.J., on a temporary basis until the Meadowlands Arena was completed, the team became the New Jersey Nets.

But NBA success, which came during the 1992–93 season under the direction of former Coach Chuck Daly, was not without disappointment. The Nets finished 43–39 and came within a game of upsetting Cleveland in the first round of the playoffs.

But within two years Daly would be gone, as would power forward Derrick Coleman and point guard Kenny Anderson. Coleman and Anderson were expected to lead the Nets to the NBA's promised land, but they each wore out their welcome in New Jersey. In 1995, Coleman was dealt to Philadelphia, while Anderson ended up in Charlotte.

The Nets now must rebuild again, this time around the interior duo of 7–6 center Shawn Bradley and power forward Jayson Williams. Swingman Ed O'Bannon and rookie guard Kerry Kittles will provide some outside scoring, but the Nets are still a long way from being contenders.

Slams It In: Jayson Williams doing what a power forward should do.

Another Garden Party

The Knicks won their first two NBA championships in 1970 and 1973, events that turned Madison Square Garden into one of the loudest arenas on earth. Although former Lakers Coach Pat Riley resigned as Knicks Coach in the summer of 1995, superstar Patrick Ewing still dominates on the court, and the Garden has started rocking again as the team looks for another championship.

It might have been the most intelligent basketball team ever to play the game, and after 48 professional seasons it's the one team New York Knicks fans have never forgotten.

A group of players that included a future United State Senator (Bill Bradley) and three future NBA head coaches (Phil Jackson, Dave DeBusschere and Willis Reed) came together in the early 1970s to produce the only two championships for a franchise that played its first professional game in 1946.

With legendary coach Red Holzman calling the shots, the Knicks destroyed opponents with a combination of skill, tenacity and discipline. They played team defense and spread the ball around an offense that had scorers at every position.

Bradley and DeBusschere manned the

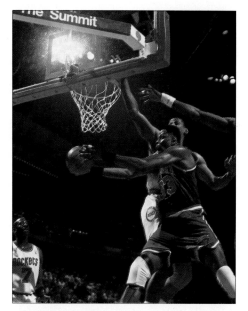

Patrick Ewing drives to the net against Houston.

forward spots, Reed played center and Walt Frazier, the flashy 6–4 guard, ran the show from out front. Jackson, who would win three NBA championships as coach of the Chicago Bulls, was a defensive stopper off the bench and known for his unselfish play.

Cazzie Russell and Dick Barnett played key roles on the 1970 Championship team while Earl Monroe, a dazzling ball handler and scorer, and Jerry Lucas came aboard for the 1973 title run. Those teams not only left a lasting impression on New Yorkers, but 20 years later Jackson applied many of Holzman's principles as coach of the Bulls.

Organized in 1946, the Knicks had a small but exciting lineup under another legendary coach, Joe Lapchick. Though the Knicks produced a string of solid seasons, they were no match for George Mikan and the Minneapolis Lakers. New York won three straight Eastern Division titles only to be defeated by Mikan's Lakers in three times in the Finals.

After that, New York didn't win a single playoff game between 1957 and 1967. But all that changed when Holzman took over midway through the 1967–68 season as he quickly molded the Knicks into an Eastern power. A championship roster came together as DeBusschere arrived via trade and Bradley returned after two years of study at Oxford. Reed had already established himself as a solid center and

ROLL OF HONOR

Conference/Division	Eastern/Atlantic			
First NBA year	1946-47			
Home Arena details	Madison Square Garden (built 1968, capacity 19,763)			
Former cities/nicknames	None			
NBA Championships	1970, 1973			
Playing Record	**G**	**W**	**L**	**Pct**
Regular Season	3883	1979	1904	.510
Playoffs (Series 33-32)	289	146	143	.505

Frazier, only a rookie on Holzman's first team, would soon become one of the NBA's greatest defensive players.

When Bill Russell retired after leading Boston to its 11th title in 13 years following the 1968–69 season, the Eastern Conference became a wide open race with the Knicks perfectly positioned. They beat Wilt Chamberlain's Los Angeles Lakers for the 1970 Championship and then won again in 1973. But as the core players aged and injuries mounted, the Knicks headed into a period of inconsistency and almost constant change.

Between 1987 and 1992, New York had six head coaches in six seasons. Superstar center Patrick Ewing, the Knicks No. 1 pick in the 1985 Draft, pushed the team to the brink of major playoff success in 1989 and 1990 only to see the franchise slip again.

But everyone seemed to know the Knicks were about to rise again. With Ewing, one of the most versatile centers ever to play the game, manning the middle, New York needed only to fill the edges.

Before the Knicks front office worried about players, however, the team decided to find a master tactician. This time the Knicks turned to another legendary coach in Pat Riley, whose Los Angeles Lakers had won four titles during the 1980s. Riley took control of a team led by Ewing, bruising power forward Charles Oakley and sharp-shooting guard John Starks. And upon Michael Jordan's brief retirement, the Eastern Conference was wide open again, and the Knicks took perfect advantage.

Led by Ewing, New York charged into the 1994 Finals only to lose a seven-game struggle with the Houston Rockets. But Riley shocked the club by resigning soon after New York's 1995 Eastern Conference Semifinal defeat by Indiana.

The Knicks have rebuilt around a nucleus of Ewing and Oakley by adding some outstanding young players, such as forward Larry Johnson and guards Allan Houston and Chris Childs. With these additions, coach Jeff Van Gundy has one of the most talented lineups in the NBA, and Ewing still has a good shot at an NBA Championship.

Charles Oakley tips in another rebound.

WALT FRAZIER
A Style All His Own

With long black sideburns and a thick mustache, Walt "Clyde" Frazier carried himself with a style that was his alone. No one dressed better than Frazier. No one had more shoes, "kicks" as he called them, or hats, known as "lids" to Frazier. His suits were colorful and among the finest made, as were his ties ("knots").

On the floor, Frazier rarely changed expressions. His 6–4, 205-pound body seemed perfectly proportioned and always under control.

A first round draft pick in 1967 by the Knicks, Frazier had been an all-around star at Southern Illinois University. Frazier made the NBA All-Defensive first team seven straight seasons starting in 1969. By 1970, his third year in the league, Frazier had become one of the cornerstones to the NBA's best team.

Given Frazier's style, the title of his first book, *Rockin' Steady*, seemed only fitting.

Orlando Magic

Penny From Heaven

Orlando struggled through its first three seasons before Shaquille O'Neal appeared. With O'Neal's arrival in 1992, the Magic improved by 20 games over the previous season. In 1994–95, with another young star on board in Anfernee "Penny" Hardaway and a veteran power forward in Horace Grant, Orlando looked like a dynasty in the making. But O'Neal has moved on, leaving the team's future in Hardaway's hands.

Magic. The name fits. How else does an rising franchise end up with consecutive No. 1 Draft picks despite a Lottery system which is weighted toward the league's worst teams?

A year after landing towering Shaquille O'Neal in the 1992 NBA Draft, Orlando won a franchise record 41 games. But the Magic finished a game short of reaching the playoffs which put them back into the league's Draft Lottery. Of the 11 Lottery teams, Orlando easily had the best record which, given the nature of the lottery, made it a 1-in-66 long shot to end up with the top pick yet again.

Then it happened. After reaching the .500 mark for the first time, the Magic were rewarded with yet another No. 1 draft choice. They chose Chris Webber, who was summarily dealt to Golden State for multi-talented guard Anfernee Hardaway plus three future No. 1 picks.

It also led to a restructuring of the Lottery system, but not before the Magic

No More Hanging Around: Shaq joins the Lakers.

had cashed in twice and, in the process, solidified the future.

All that was fine with front office

dynamo Pat Williams, who had already provided the franchise with a solid foundation. One of the NBA's finest promoters, Williams arrived in Orlando after a nearly 20-year education that started with the Chicago Bulls in 1969. In the mid 1980s, he departed to help bring a franchise to an Orlando community known primarily as the home to Disney World.

Williams' magic helped land one of four new expansion franchises and the team began play, along with Minnesota, in 1989. Not unexpectedly, Orlando struggled through a difficult first season, losing 64 games with aging veterans such as Reggie Theus, Sidney Green and Dave Corzine occupying roster spots.

The Magic improved quickly, however, behind young and talented players such as Dennis Scott and Nick Anderson. But a series of injuries buried Orlando during the 1991–92 season and the team slipped to 61 losses and the NBA's second worst record.

The silver lining turned out to be the 1992 Draft which featured one of the most imposing centers in years in O'Neal. At 7–1 and 301 pounds, O'Neal had the ability and presence to redirect an entire franchise. And that's what he did in Orlando. O'Neal averaged 23.4 points, 13.8 rebounds and blocked more than three shots a game in his first NBA season. That, however, was only the beginning.

Hardaway added yet another dimension to a fast-rising franchise. Then, what many considered the final piece arrived when Horace Grant signed with the Magic.

R O L L	O F	H O N O R		
Conference/Division	Eastern/Atlantic			
First NBA year	1989-90			
Home Arena details	Orlando Arena (built 1989, capacity 15,291)			
Former cities/nicknames	None			
NBA Championships	None			
Playing Record	G	W	L	Pct
Regular Season	574	278	296	.484
Playoffs (Series 5-3)	36	18	18	.500

HORACE GRANT
Three Ring Leader

Until Horace Grant arrived in Orlando prior to the 1994–95 season, Shaquille O'Neal had a problem. Try as he might, not even O'Neal could control the Magic's inside game by himself. And although O'Neal and the rest of the young Orlando roster had improved dramatically, the team still needed a veteran to show the way.

Enter Grant.

After helping the Chicago Bulls to three consecutive championships with his solid defense and rebounding, Grant signed with Orlando as a free agent in 1994. That move, coupled with Orlando's improved play, turned the franchise into an instant championship contender.

Not only does Grant know how to win in the playoffs, something the Magic hadn't done prior to 1995, but he has become the perfect complement to O'Neal under the basket. Grant gives Orlando another rebounder, but it's his defense that stands out.

"Horace understands the importance of defense," says former Bulls coach John Bach. "And he's not afraid of doing what it takes to get the job done."

In 1994, Grant was named to the NBA All-Defensive Second Team.

Orlando finished the season as the Eastern Conference's top team and went all the way to the 1995 NBA Finals. However, Houston ended the Magic's run in four straight games.

1996 saw the Magic make another run at the NBA Finals, only to lose to Bulls in the Eastern Conference Finals. That was to be the last hurrah for Shaq in Orlando, as he headed for the Lakers in the off-season. Without O'Neal, it will take a real magic act for Orlando to reach the NBA Finals again.

Worth Every Penny: Anfernee Hardaway soars in for a slam.

Looking for Another House Call

The Philadelphia 76ers rode Julius "Dr. J" Erving's brilliance to the 1983 NBA Championship. But after trading superstar Charles Barkley and revamping the roster from the bottom up, Philadelphia has turned the future over to guards Jerry Stackhouse and Allen Iverson and forward Clarence Weatherspoon. If the 76ers are going to rekindle title hopes, they'll have to do it with those three leading the way.

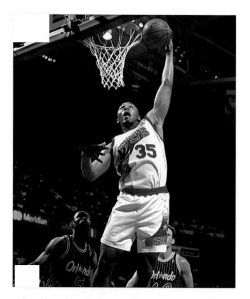

The "Spoon" dishes up a slam against Orlando.

The Philadelphia 76ers have done just about everything at least once. From winning NBA championships to recording the single worst season in league history and trading away two of basketball's most accomplished players, Philadelphia has long been one of the NBA's more colorful creations.

The team started out as the Syracuse Nationals and didn't arrive in Philadelphia until 1963. Indeed, the 76ers were born out of the void created by the Philadelphia Warriors, who moved to San Francisco. In the 32 years since, the 76ers have usually been one of the league's foremost

attractions for one reason or another.

The franchise is also considered largely responsible for the creation of the 24-second clock. In an intrasquad game prior to the 1954–55 season, Syracuse owner Danny Biasone improvised an early forerunner of the current shot clock. He decided on 24 seconds as an experimental time guide for offensive possessions. The experiment proved to be a success and the NBA adopted Biasone's idea as a league rule, which resulted in a faster, more high-scoring game.

Those early Syracuse teams also had two of the era's finest players in Dolph Schayes and Johnny "Red" Kerr. With the addition of rookie Earl Lloyd prior to the 1954–55 season, the Nationals won their only championship.

Once in Philadelphia, however, the franchise became a league-wide show. San Francisco grudgingly agreed to trade Wilt Chamberlain to the 76ers midway through the 1964–65 season. One year later, Philadelphia had a starting lineup loaded with talent. Chamberlain, Billy Cunningham, Chet Walker, Hal Greer and Wali Jones helped the 76ers to a brilliant 68–13 regular season record, second best in history.

With Chamberlain passing more than earlier in his career, Philadelphia ended Boston's string of eight straight NBA titles by eliminating the Celtics in the playoffs. The 76ers went on to beat San Francisco in the 1967 Finals for their first Philadelphia title.

Less than two years later, however, Chamberlain was shipped off to the Lakers and the 76ers self-destructed. They lost a

DERRICK COLEMAN
Time to Shine

The praise has been nearly drowned out by the whispers. Coleman could be one of the league's best players — if he wanted to be.

He has always had amazing potential. He can play a dominant power game inside, or step outside and hit the jumper. He can run the floor and block shots. He can throw court-length overhand passes with either hand.

Still, Coleman has not capitalized on his potential. After winning the 1991 NBA Rookie of the Year award in New Jersey, he averaged 20.7 points and 11.2 rebounds in 1993 and seemed on the verge of being an MVP candidate and a perennial All-Star.

But a string of injuries and a lack of conditioning cost Coleman several games in 1994, and by 1995 the Nets were looking to trade him. Philadelphia was happy to pick Coleman up, but an ankle injury kept him out of the lineup much of the season.

Now, at the age of 29, Coleman must prove himself all over again. He has the talent, but he must show that he has the desire.

ROLL OF HONOR

Conference/Division	Eastern/Atlantic			
First NBA year	1949-50			
Home Arena details	Core States Center (built 1996, capacity 21,000)			
Former cities/nicknames	Syracuse Nationals (1949-63)			
NBA Championships	1955, 1967, 1983			

Playing Record	G	W	L	Pct
Regular Season	3712	2035	1677	.548
Playoffs (Series 36-34)	328	175	153	.534

record 73 games during the 1972–73 season. But within four years the team again had one of the most exciting rosters in the league with Julius Erving, George McGinnis, Doug Collins, Steve Mix and young Darryl Dawkins carrying Philadelphia into the 1977 NBA Finals.

Behind Erving's brilliant play and the coaching of Cunningham, the 76ers were one of the elite teams in the league along with the Lakers and the Celtics in the early 1980s. The era produced only a single title (1983), however, as the Lakers and Celtics started to dominate.

Charles Barkley arrived in 1984 and the 76ers remained a solid team capable of beating anyone. But Erving eventually slowed down and Philadelphia slowed with him. Following Barkley's trade in 1992 the 76ers lost 56 games.

The future, as far as owner Harold Katz believed, arrived in 1993. Philadelphia used the No. 2 pick to select 7–6 center Shawn Bradley, who was quickly given uniform No. 76. The Bradley era was short-lived, however. The big center did not live up to his potential and was sent to New Jersey for Derrick Coleman, who was also a disappointment, suffering an ankle injury that has limited his production. Coleman, former No. 1 pick in the NBA Draft, now finds the top pick in the 1996 NBA Draft—Allen Iverson—as his teammate. Iverson, a cat-quick point guard, and Coleman join the underrated Clarence Weatherspoon—a Barkley clone—and explosive guard Jerry Stackhouse in attempting to return the Sixers to their past standing.

· ·

Jerry Stackhouse flying towards the basket.

59

Home of the Rising Suns

For years the Phoenix Suns had been one of the Western Conference's top teams. They even made an appearance in the 1976 NBA Finals. But the Suns never won more than 57 regular season games until Charles Barkley rode into town prior to the 1992–93 season. The Suns won a franchise-record 62 games and reached the 1993 Finals, this time losing to Chicago. The Suns have risen, but can they finally win a championship?

For years the first pick in the NBA draft was determined by the simple toss of a coin. Representatives from the worst teams in the Eastern and Western Conferences would gather for the annual coin flip.

As the Phoenix Suns can attest, being lucky usually translates into being good. The Suns entered the league along with Milwaukee in 1968. Both teams limped through difficult first seasons, Phoenix relying on sharp shooting guards Gail Goodrich and Dick Van Arsdale and not much else. Over in the East, the Bucks had similar problems.

As a result, Phoenix and Milwaukee ended up squaring off in the coin toss. This one, however, had historic implications that both franchises understood. The Suns won the right to call the toss and called

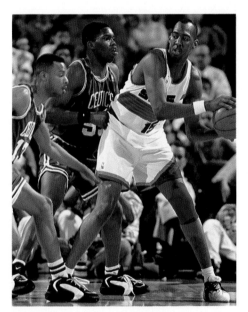

Danny Manning ready for action.

ROLL OF HONOR

Conference/Division	Western/Pacific		
First NBA year	1968-69		
Home Arena details	America West Arena (dedicated 1992, capacity 19,023)		
Former cities/nicknames	None		
NBA Championships	None		

Playing Record	G	W	L	Pct
Regular Season	2296	1246	1050	.543
Playoffs (Series 20-18)	176	87	89	.494

heads. The coin came up tails, Lew Alcindor (now Kareem Abdul-Jabbar) went to Milwaukee and within two seasons the Bucks had an NBA title.

What about the Suns? It has been a

struggle often frustrated by stinging losses in the playoffs.

Just a year after that inaugural season, Phoenix extended the Los Angeles Lakers to seven games in the Western Division semifinals, a remarkable turnaround aided by playground legend Connie Hawkins.

Although it would be six years before Phoenix reached the playoffs again, the building process remained impressive. By 1976 the team had assembled the best team in the West with young stars such as Paul Westphal, the former Suns coach, Alvan Adams, Garfield Heard and Curtis Perry along with veterans like Van Arsdale and Keith Erickson.

A 42–40 regular season finish set up a dramatic postseason that included what many think is the best playoff game in NBA history. Phoenix beat Seattle in the Western Conference Semifinals and then upset defending champion Golden State to reach the Finals.

And that's where the real drama began. Matched against the powerful Boston Celtics, the Suns won two of the first four games to set up a crucial Game 5 at Boston. The contest took three overtime periods and rolled along at a numbing pace. It took Heard's incredible, high-arching jump shot with one second left in the second overtime to force yet a third extra period. Ultimately, Boston's deep bench and veteran cool prevailed and the Celtics went on to close out the title in six games.

But the Suns had established themselves under coach John MacLeod. Players such as Westphal, Adams and Walter Davis made Phoenix one of the West's top teams for years. But the Suns wouldn't make a return trip to the Finals until Charles Barkley arrived prior the 1992–93 season.

With Westphal assuming the coaching reigns and Barkley taking over the scoring and rebounding, Phoenix rolled through the 1992–93 season. And this time no one stopped them until Chicago and Michael Jordan in the NBA Finals.

The Suns have been unable to return to the Finals since then. Injuries to point guard Kevin Johnson, versatile forward Danny Manning and Barkley have forced the Suns to limp into the playoffs without their best lineup on the floor. A pair of young guards, Wesley Person and Michael Finley, have injected life into the attack, and Barkley remains a man on a mission. The Suns haven't set yet.

Passing Fancy: One of the NBA's greatest point guards, Kevin Johnson keys the Suns' attack.

BLAZERS™

One Brief Shining Moment

It happened in 1977 when center Bill Walton found the strength and physical good fortune to last an entire season. The Trail Blazers won the only championship in franchise history, an improbable romp past the Philadelphia 76ers. Since then, however, near misses on and off the court have left Portland looking for yet another chance.

Despite years of success and two recent trips to the NBA Finals, the Portland franchise is marked by two events that came seven years apart.

The first happened in 1977 when a Trail Blazers team led by legendary center Bill Walton and bruising forward Maurice Lucas marched through an unlikely, yet brilliant postseason en route the franchise's

Passing the Buck: Buck Williams is now clearing off rebounds for the New York Knicks.

only NBA Championship.

The team had joined the NBA in 1971 along with expansion franchises in Buffalo and Cleveland. Lenny Wilkens took over the coaching duties in 1974, which was also his last season as a player.

Wilkens lasted two seasons before management turned the team over to Jack Ramsay. A great coach in his own right, Ramsay received the gift of his career when Walton stayed healthy enough to last through the 1976–77 season.

Teamed with Lucas and a rag-tag collection of hard-working players, Walton turned the Trail Blazers into champions. Walton led the league in rebounding (14.4) and blocked shots (3.25) and his passing helped ignite the league's third best offense.

But after breezing through the first three rounds of the 1976 playoffs, Portland ran hard into Julius Erving and the Philadelphia 76ers in the Finals. Philadelphia took a quick 2–0 lead and as the series shifted to Portland, many thought the Trail Blazers were simply overmatched.

That's when Portland exploded, winning the next two games by 22 and 32 points and forever shifting the momentum. The Trail Blazers went on to win four straight games and claim their first and only NBA title. The championship run not only shocked the rest of the league, but it make a folk hero out of Walton.

Able to defend, pass and score as well as any big man in the league, Walton appeared

---

★ ★ ★ ★ ★ ★ ★ ★ ★ ★ ★

BILL WALTON
Two Feet Short

The pain in Bill Walton's feet could be felt throughout the entire NBA. One of the greatest college players in the history of basketball, Walton figured to be at least that good as a professional.

He could shoot, defend, run the floor and pass as well as any big man in the game. So when Portland acquired Walton in the 1974 Draft, the league took notice.

Though Walton's performance never disappointed, his body failed miserably. Foot injuries limited him to 35 games as a rookie and just 51 games his second season. Walton stayed healthy enough to play 65 games during the 1976–77 season, however, and then carried on through the playoffs.

Walton averaged 18.2 points, 15.2 rebounds, blocked more than three shots a game and helped direct the Portland offense. The Trail Blazers overcame Philadelphia to win the 1977 NBA championship.

Although Walton's career would continue to be marked by injuries, he did win another NBA title with Boston in 1986.

when P.J. Carlesimo took over as head coach. Then, in early 1995, Drexler was dealt to Houston.

The 1995–96 season saw the Portland debut of Arvydas Sabonis, the extremely talented Lithuanian center who was one of the best players in Europe during the 1980s. Sabonis, now 31 and hobbled by past injuries, was able to turn back the clock and lead the Blazers into the playoffs. He hasn't made anyone forget Walton's glory days, but he has inspired hope for the future.

ABOVE Cliff Robinson: They shall not pass. RIGHT Arvydas Sabonis: Lithuanian lift-off.

to be the kind of player that could carry an entire franchise. Once considered a solid but thin team, Portland was now seen as a team on the rise with a potentially dominating player leading the ascension.

Portland was even better the following season, but Walton's foot problems ended any chance of another title. His season ended two games into the playoffs and eventually, so too did his future in Portland. Walton missed the entire 1978–79 season and a year later was shipped off to the San Diego Clippers.

Portland had a chance to take another giant leap forward in 1984. A previous trade had given Portland, 48–34 in the 1983–84 season, the No. 2 pick in the 1984 Draft.

But with it came a decision that will forever haunt the franchise. After Houston selected Hakeem Olajuwon with the first choice, Portland decided to gamble on 7–1 center Sam Bowie. Chicago then used the third pick to grab Michael Jordan.

With a young Clyde Drexler set to take over the shooting guard spot and Kiki Vandweghe the team's leading scorer at small forward, Portland lacked only a solid big man in the middle.

But Bowie had missed two entire seasons during college at the University of Kentucky with leg problems. Though no one figured Jordan would become the game's brightest star, everyone knew about Bowie's medical problems. And Portland paid dearly for what turned out to be a horrible mistake. Bowie missed 44 games his second season, 77 his third and then

didn't play at all his fourth year in the league.

As with Walton, however, Portland survived Bowie's injuries. Indeed, the franchise corrected itself quickly and entered the 1990s as the West's dominant team. Led by Drexler, Terry Porter, Jerome Kersey and Buck Williams, the Trail Blazers reached the NBA Finals in 1990 and 1992 only to lose hard-fought championship rounds against Detroit and then Chicago.

Portland began to remake itself again prior to the 1994–95 season

ROLL OF HONOR

Conference/Division	Western/Pacific		
First NBA year	1970-71		
Home Arena details	Rose Garden (built 1995, capacity 21,500)		
Former cities/nicknames	None		
NBA Championships	1977		

Playing Record	G	W	L	Pct
Regular Season	2132	1129	1003	.530
Playoffs (Series 14-18)	144	69	75	.479

The Traveling Kings

They have moved across the country with stops in Rochester, Cincinnati, Kansas City and finally Sacramento, but the Kings still haven't found the road to the NBA Finals. But since settling in Sacramento, the Kings have started to assemble a roster capable of making a run at the playoffs. In 1995–96, the Kings finally hit postseason paydirt.

Consider the cross-country odyssey that landed the Kings in Sacramento. It does provide perspective. The Sacramento Kings used to be the Kansas City Kings who used to be the Kansas City-Omaha Kings who used to be the Cincinnati Royals who were originally the Rochester Royals. There was even a brief life before that in the Midwest.

If that's not enough, consider the disparate group of players on that first team. Future pro football Hall of Fame quarterback Otto Graham, eventual television star Chuck Connors, future New York Knicks coach Red Holzman and long-time

major league baseball player Del Rice were all members of the 1946 team that won the National Basketball League title. Not surprisingly, the team was located elsewhere, in Sheboygan, Wisconsin, during that championship season.

Rochester joined the NBA in 1948 and immediately became one of the strongest franchises. By their third season, the Royals were playing for the NBA title thanks to players such as Arnie Risen and Bob Davies.

The Royals, and later the Kings, would never reach another championship series. That might have changed had the career of Maurice Stokes not been cut short by tragedy. Stokes arrived in the 1955 Draft and was developing into a top player when he contracted a crippling brain disease called encephalitis.

A year earlier, in 1957, the team had moved to Cincinnati in part because management wanted to claim the great Oscar Robertson with a territorial pick in the 1960 Draft.

Robertson, star of the U.S. men's team in the 1960 Rome Olympics, joined the team for the 1960–61 season. Robertson averaged an incredible 30.8 points, 12.3 rebounds and 11.5 assists per game during the 1961–62 season. No player has even come close to averaging double figures in

Rejection: Sacramento's Brian Grant leaps to turn away a field goal attempt.

MITCH RICHMOND
King of the Kings

Everybody wanted to know which opponent Michael Jordan considered the toughest to play against. To the surprise of many, Jordan usually answered Mitch Richmond.

"He's almost as big (6–5, 215 pounds) as me, he's strong and he can do many of things I can do," said Jordan. "He's also one of the few guys that plays both ends of the court like me."

The No. 5 pick in the 1988 Draft, Richmond was picked by Golden State. Then, after a brilliant season in 1990–91, Golden State gambled and sent Richmond to Sacramento for rookie Billy Owens.

Richmond never missed a beat, leading the Kings in scoring in each of his first two seasons. He went into the 1993–94 season with a 22.5 points per game career scoring average and remained one of the best pure shooting guards the league has ever seen. After making his All-Star debut in the 1994 game in Minneapolis, Richmond was named Most Valuable Player of the 1995 All-Star Game in Phoenix and was a member of the 1996 U.S. Olympic team.

any three statistical categories much less a player who stood 6–5 and played guard.

But not even Robertson could carry the Royals past Bill Russell's Boston Celtics.

From there, however, the franchise lapsed into a 26-year period marked by moves and mediocrity. It moved West and became the Kansas City-Omaha Kings and, four years later, the Kansas City Kings.

The team's only real playoff success came unexpectedly following the 1980–81 season. With Otis Birdsong, Scott Wedman and Phil Ford doing all the scoring, the Kings just made the playoffs with a 40–42 regular season record.

But after knocking off Portland in the First Round, the Kings shocked Pacific Division champion Phoenix in a rousing seven-game series. They were eventually eliminated by the Houston Rockets in the Western Conference finals.

By 1985 the Kings were on the move again, this time landing in Sacramento. The Kings appeared headed out of their dark age until injuries beat them down again.

Still, with young talent like Mitch Richmond, Walt Williams, Bobby Hurley, Brian Grant, Michael Smith and Lionel Simmons, Sacramento improved by 11 games in 1994–95. The Kings added point guard Tyus Edney to the mix in 1995–96 and made it to the playoffs, where they challenged Seattle before bowing out in the first round. Sacramento added another scoring weapon by acquiring guard Mahmoud Abdul-Rauf prior to the 1996–97 season as the Kings look to go even farther into the playoffs.

· ·

Mitch Richmond sees an opening.

R O L L   O F   H O N O R

Conference/Division	Western/Pacific			
First NBA year	1948-49			
Home Arena details	ARCO Arena (built 1988, capacity 17,317)			
Former cities/nicknames	Rochester Royals (1948-57), Cincinnati Royals (1957-72), Kansas-City-Omaha Kings (1972-75)			
NBA Championships	1951			

Playing Record	G	W	L	Pct
Regular Season	3777	1731	2046	.458
Playoffs (Series 9-20)	118	46	72	.390

SAN ANTONIO SPURS

A Tale of Two Players

Few teams won more creatively than the San Antonio Spurs of the late 1970s and early 1980s. They led the league in scoring by connecting from just about anywhere on the court. But they never reached a single championship series. Now the responsibility for carrying the franchise rests with 7–1 center David Robinson, a former Naval officer nicknamed "The Admiral."

They will be remembered as the greatest two players in the Spurs' history. Unfortunately for San Antonio, by the time David Robinson and George Gervin ended on the same bench, one was playing while the other coached.

Look back to the league's most dominant championship teams and all of them had an inside-outside attack.

Unfortunately for Robinson and Gervin, the two championship components never intersected. Gervin ended a brilliant 12-year career in San Antonio four years before Robinson arrived and so far, neither has an NBA title to show for all their wondrous talents.

The Spurs started out as the Dallas Chaparrals in the ABA. Though Dallas had immediate success on the court, winning 46 games its first season, the franchise was a box office disaster. The team eventually became the Texas Chaparrals and alternated home games between Dallas, Fort Worth and Lubbock.

Then, in 1973, San Antonio businessman Red McCombs bought the franchise, moved it to his home town and renamed it the Spurs. Prior to the 1973–74 season, McCombs also spent more than $500,000, an enormous sum then, to buy Gervin and center Swen Nater from Virginia.

Gervin, a slender 6–7 scoring machine, had a dazzling array of hooks, scoops, jumpers and dunks. By the time San Antonio joined the NBA in 1976, Gervin

Glad To Be Back: Sean Elliott

had four professional seasons behind him and a fully-developed offensive arsenal.

With Gervin winning four scoring titles in five years, the Spurs became one of the most explosive teams in history. But without an impact player at center, Gervin's heroics weren't enough. San Antonio reached the Western Conference Finals under Coach Stan Albeck in 1982 and 1983 but couldn't get past the Los Angeles Lakers.

San Antonio didn't return to form until Robinson arrived in 1989. The Spurs had

SEAN ELLIOTT
No Place Like Home

After four solid seasons in San Antonio — including one All-Star appearance — Sean Elliott was shocked when the Spurs traded him to Detroit for forward Dennis Rodman in 1993. Elliott, a sharp-shooting small forward, had found a home on the perimeter of the Spurs offense. When opposing defenses collapsed on David Robinson, Elliott was open for three-point bombs.

In Detroit, without a dominant big man, Elliott never found his stride. His 12.1 points in 1993–94 was his lowest average since his rookie year, and Elliott was miserable on a rebuilding team.

He longed to return to San Antonio, and the Pistons granted him his wish by sending him back to the Spurs after just one season. Rejuvinated, Elliott became an even bigger offensive factor in his second San Antonio stint. He became a more accurate three-point shooter and added a variety of slashing moves to the basket to his bag of tricks.

The Spurs appear to have learned their lesson. They aren't likely to part with Elliott again anytime soon.

used the No. 1 pick in 1987 to draft Robinson, who had to fulfill a military commitment before he could join the team.

ROLL OF HONOR

Conference/Division	Western/Midwest			
First NBA year	1976-77 (ABA 1967-68)			
Home Arena details	Alamodome (built 1993, capacity 20,500)			
Former cities/nicknames	Dallas Chaparrals (1967-70, 1971-73),			
	Texas Chaparrals (1970-71)			
NBA Championships	None			
Playing Record	G	W	L	Pct
NBA Regular Season	1640	914	726	.558
NBA/ABA combined	2384	1288	1092	.540
NBA Playoffs (series 8-17)	119	52	67	.437
NBA/ABA combined	168	69	99	.418

When he arrived Robinson lived up to the expectations. Robinson not only helped San Antonio improve from 21 to 56 victories in his first season, but the Spurs narrowly missed the Western Conference Finals. Portland needed two overtime victories, the second in a grueling Game 7, to eliminate San Antonio in the 1990 Western Conference Semifinals.

It took time for the Spurs to return to that level. Injuries to starters Terry Cummings and Willie Anderson stunted the team's progress. Then numerous coaching changes sent the franchise spinning until former player John Lucas took over 21 games into the 1992–93 campaign.

Lucas immediately turned to Robinson, who carried San Antonio back into the Conference Semifinals. The team added Dennis Rodman prior to the 1993–94 season and Cummings and Anderson appeared recovered from their injuries. Then, prior to the 1994–95 season, Bob Hill took over the team's head coaching duties and Sean Elliott returned in a trade.

The Spurs responded by winning a club record 62 games and the Midwest Division title, while Robinson was named the NBA's MVP. The Spurs reached the Western Conference Finals before falling to Houston.

The Spurs traded Rodman to Chicago to improve team chemistry, but were unable to advance any farther in the playoffs in 1996. But with the Admiral and Co. gaining additional postseason experience, the Spurs are close to a breakthrough.

The Admiral Takes Command: David Robinson throws down a lefthanded slam on the Bucks.

Blasting Off Again

The Seattle SuperSonics appeared to be on their way to a dubious distinction: best regular-season team in the NBA. Despite stellar seasons in 1994 and 1995, the Sonics had lost in the first round of the NBA Playoffs. All that changed in 1996, as Shawn Kemp and Gary Payton led the Sonics to their first NBA Finals appearance since 1979.

The SuperSonics had made it to the Western Conference Finals in 1993, but couldn't duplicate their postseason success in the next two seasons. Seattle fans hope that their team will lead them to their first NBA Championship in nearly two decades.

Indeed, Coach George Karl can only hope the experience pays off like it did for Lenny Wilkens' squad. Wilkens, who had been a player/coach for Seattle in the early 1970s, returned to the bench early in the 1977–78 season. Wilkens immediately transformed the franchise into a winner.

Seattle had come into the league in 1967, but had only limited success until Wilkens' arrival in 1969. As the Sonics' point guard, he guided the team to 47 victories during the 1971–72 season but, incredibly, the team failed to make the playoffs.

Former Boston Celtics great Bill Russell coached the team for four seasons and led Seattle to its first playoff appearance in 1975. But Russell's hard-edged approach didn't wear well. Before long, owner Sam Schulman was digging in his files for another leader.

That's where he found Wilkens, who had since retired as a player. Wilkens returned to his former team and quickly molded players Gus Williams, Dennis Johnson, rookie Jack Sikma, reserve Freddie Brown and Marvin Webster into a title contender.

The SuperSonics rolled through the early rounds of the playoffs before meeting Washington. A seven-game championship battle ended with the Bullets taking the 1978 championship on Seattle's home court, something no one forgot when the two teams met again a year later.

Shawn Kemp leaves the opposition standing.

Although Webster, a towering center, left the team for New York following the Finals, the SuperSonics never missed a beat. They received bulky Lonnie Shelton from the Knicks as compensation for Webster and turned the center spot over to Sikma.

By the time the SuperSonics returned to the Finals in 1979 not even the Bullets had a chance. Seattle eliminated Washington in a quick five-game series for the franchise's first championship.

The team remained solid through the next 12 seasons, but never quite as good as it was under Wilkens. Players such as Tom Chambers, Xavier McDaniel and Dale Ellis helped keep the team competitive. Then, midway through the 1991–92 season, Coach George Karl took over and the

ROLL OF HONOR

Conference/Division	Western/Pacific			
First NBA year	1967-68			
Home Arena details	Key Arena (built 1995, capacity 17,800)			
Former cities/nicknames	None			
NBA Championships	1979			
Playing Record	**G**	**W**	**L**	**Pct**
Regular Season	2378	1253	1125	.527
Playoffs (Series 16-15)	153	74	79	.484

SuperSonics' roster came together.

Combining veterans Eddie Johnson and Ricky Pierce with youngsters Shawn Kemp, Derrick McKey and Gary Payton, Karl turned the SuperSonics into an end-to-end menace. Seattle then traded for veteran center Sam Perkins just after the 1993 All-Star break. Suddenly, the SuperSonics were ready to make their run. Kemp, one of the NBA's rising superstars, averaged 17.8 points and more than 10 rebounds a game. But it was defense that keyed the Seattle charge as they became the only team in the league to finish among the top five in scoring and defense.

The SuperSonics knocked off Western Conference rivals Utah and Houston before extending Phoenix to Game 7 in the 1993 Western Conference Finals.

If Seattle learned anything it's that the team needed just a little more help, particularly in the starting lineup. In two quick, if not brilliant moves, the SuperSonics added 6–5 guard Kendall Gill in a trade with Charlotte and then 6–10 forward Detlef Schrempf in a deal with Indiana.

Schrempf provided veteran leadership on the frontline, while Gill, among the league's most versatile guards, added another dimension out front. Both became perfect additions to the full-court attack that turned Seattle into the league's best team during the 1993–94 regular season. But a stunning loss to Denver in the First Round of the 1994 Playoffs ended a spectacular season. The same scenario was repeated in 1994–95 when a strong season ended in a first-round loss in the Playoffs.

In 1995–96, Seattle broke of its playoff slump and surged to the NBA Finals, only to lose to Chicago, 4–2.

Lesson learned, it's now time for another title run.

DETLEF SCHREMPF
Back Home Again

The tattoo just over Detlef Schrempf's heart shows, among other things, an eagle spreading its wings. For Schrempf, the image has meaning. "It has more to do with inner strength," he says.

And that's something Schrempf knows about. After a solid career at the University of Washington, Schrempf was the first-round pick of the Dallas Mavericks in 1985. His style was supposed to be perfect for the rapidly rising Mavericks. Instead, Schrempf suffered through three disappointing seasons in Dallas before being traded to Indiana.

Schrempf blossomed into an All-Star in Indiana and twice was named the league's best Sixth Man. When he moved into the Pacers' starting lineup in 1992–93, he became an All-Star for the first time registering career bests in total rebounds, assists, points and steals.

By the time Schrempf was dealt to Seattle in 1993, he had become one of the league's best all-around players.

Super SuperSonic: Gary Payton

© 1994 NBAP

Building on A History of Success

Isiah Thomas led the Detroit Pistons to two NBA Championships as a player. Now, Thomas will try to build a winner from the ground up in Toronto. If history is any guide, then Thomas and guard Damon Stoudamire can be expected to get the job done.

Isiah Thomas' basketball résumé is as long as the Toronto Raptors' is short. At every level and without exception, Thomas has distinguished himself and the teams he's been associated with as winners.

As a college sophomore, Thomas led Indiana University to the NCAA Championship. In the NBA, as one of the most dynamic point guards to ever play the game, Thomas guided Detroit to back-to-back NBA titles. So when Toronto team president John Bitove went looking for the man to lead the expansion Raptors, the decision was an easy one.

"The two things that came through over and over were that Thomas is incredibly intelligent and he's driven to be successful," says Bitove.

As vice president of basketball operations for the Raptors, Thomas will need every ounce of experience he gained during his brilliant NBA career to make Toronto competitive. The Raptors, which along with the Vancouver Grizzlies make their NBA debut in the 1995–96 season, will play in the rugged Central Division which includes playoff-caliber teams such as the Indiana Pacers, Chicago Bulls and Atlanta Hawks.

That's one reason Thomas wasted no time before studying some of the most successful coaches and front office people in professional sports. He found out how coaches such as Don Shula of NFL's Miami Dolphins built that franchise into a power. And he talked to NBA veterans, includ-

Damon Stoudamire: 1996 Rookie of the Year

ing former Pistons coach Chuck Daly and all-time great Bill Russell.

"I confirmed a gut feeling I had that being an expansion team, that if you wanted to win a championship and you depended strictly on the rules, then it's going to take you a long time to do that," said Thomas. "You've got to be imaginative, be creative. The Dallas Cowboys, when they came in, started drafting basketball players, baseball players, people they looked at in a totally different paradigm. They made a shift in sports that football hadn't taken then. They had to change the game, the

DAMON STOUDAMIRE
Toronto's Leading Man

There were other players available when the Toronto Raptors made the seventh choice in the 1995 NBA Draft. But Isiah Thomas had his eyes fixed on one man.

Indeed, Thomas no doubt recognized a bit of himself in Damon Stoudamire, the Raptors first-round pick. Though just 5-foot-10, Stoudamire was a three-time All Pac-10 player with exactly the kind of skills that made Thomas a perennial NBA All-Star.

Stoudamire worked hard to prove himself as an NBA rookie. He was second in the league in minutes played, singlehandedly keeping the Raptors in games they would have otherwise had no chance to win. He finished the season averaging 19 points and 9.3 assists. For his efforts, Stoudamire was named 1996 NBA Rookie of the Year.

Like his childhood hero, Nate "Tiny" Archibald, Stoudamire is a point guard with the ability to pass and score with equal success. Thomas is glad the Raptors were able to make Stoudamire the cornerstone of his franchise.

"This is the guy we wanted all along," says Thomas. "He definitely fits our style."

And he appears to fit the NBA style as well.

way people thought."

Which is exactly what Thomas did when the Toronto made its first choice in the 1995 NBA Draft. Instead of drafting a big man with the No. 7 pick, Thomas took defied conventional wisdom and chose point guard Damon Stoudamire. As it turned out, that was just one of many moves orchestrated by Thomas.

Former Chicago Bulls guard B. J. Armstrong, was selected first by the Raptors in the expansion draft, but with the selection of Stoudamire there was talk of trading Armstrong to a contender for some frontcourt players to add to veterans Oliver Miller, Ed Pinckney, Acie Earl, John Salley, Doug Smith, Zan Tabak, Tony Massenburg, Jerome Kersey and Dontonio Wingfield, all of whom were selected in the expansion draft. Others arriving through the expansion draft were Willie Anderson B. J. Tyler, Keith Jennings and Andres Guibert.

Some of those players did not make it through the Raptors' first season, while some blossomed. Stoudamire outperformed all expectations, earning NBA Rookie of the Year honors. Swingman Tracy Murray made the most of his opportunity by averaging 16.2 points and developing into one of the NBA's top sixth men.

The Raptors' first coach, Brendan Malone, exited after the 1995–96 season. He is replaced by Darrell Walker, a former NBA guard known for his defensive play. If Thomas can continue to improve the lineup Walker has to work with—as he did by drafting versatile forward/center Marcus Camby with the No. 2 pick in the 1996 NBA Draft—the Raptors could become an expansion story in a hurry.

Tracy Murray joins Washington's frontcourt.

ROLL OF HONOR

Conference/Division	Eastern/Central
First NBA year	1995–96
Home Arena details	SkyDome (built 1989, capacity 23,000)
Former cities/nicknames	None
NBA Championships	None

Playing Record	G	W	L	Pct
Regular Season	82	21	61	.256
Playoffs	None			

The Jazz Age

The name belongs to another city, but the results are Utah's alone. Riding the remarkable talents of superstars John Stockton and Karl Malone, the Jazz haven't missed the playoffs since 1983. But if the Utah hopes to map out a championship run it's going to need more than a dynamic duo to get the job done.

In a city best known for the Mormon Tabernacle, the nickname of the state's only major professional sports franchise doesn't fit. Then again, no one figured the New Orleans Jazz would one day be situated in Salt Lake City, Utah.

When the team became the NBA's 18th franchise in 1974 it was situated in New Orleans, a town known for its music as its 24-hour clubs. Given the sensibilities of the respective communities, the Jazz couldn't have endured a greater culture shock when the franchise moved to Utah in 1979.

But it had been a rocky start in New Orleans, where the team had five coaches in its first five seasons. Management had also gambled heavily on local legend "Pistol" Pete Maravich, one of the greatest showmen the game has ever known.

Maravich had become a college basket-

The Jazz surround San Antonio's David Robinson.

ball legend at Louisiana State University and management, banking on Maravich's drawing power, wanted him back home. The Jazz put together an elaborate package of players and draft picks to obtain Maravich from the Atlanta Hawks for New Orleans' first season.

After a difficult debut, the Jazz quickly became respectable thanks in large part to Maravich. The 6–5 guard, who handled the ball as well as any player in history, was twice named to the All-NBA first

ROLL OF HONOR

Conference/Division	Western/Midwest			
First NBA year	1974-75			
Home Arena details	Delta Center (built 1991, capacity 19,911)			
Former cities/nicknames	New Orleans Jazz (1974-79)			
NBA Championships	None			
Playing Record	G	W	L	Pct
Regular Season	1804	917	887	.508
Playoffs (Series 10-13)	117	55	62	.470

team during his five seasons with the Jazz. Maravich led the league in scoring in 1976–77 and once drilled the New York Knicks for 68 points in a single game.

But the Pistol wasn't enough to keep the franchise from moving west. It wasn't until Frank Layden assumed control in 1981 that the Jazz started making some noise, and in 1983–84, the team reached the playoffs for the first time.

With virtually total control of the roster, Layden went to work molding exactly the kind of team he wanted. Starting with a nucleus that included Adrian Dantley, Darrell Griffith and Danny Schayes, Layden pushed and pulled the team to its first winning season. By 1984, he had added Thurl Bailey and 7–4 Mark Eaton, who had been discovered by a UCLA assistant coach while working as an automobile mechanic.

With a Midwest Division title also coming that season, the Jazz had arrived. Staying among the elite, however, proved difficult until Utah made the two most important draft choices in franchise history.

The Jazz used a first-round pick to select point guard John Stockton in 1984 and a year later used another for 6–9 forward Karl Malone. Since Malone's arrival, Utah went into the 1994–95 season without a single losing season.

Indeed, Malone and Stockton have developed into an ideal inside-outside combination. Although the Jazz have operated without the benefit of a top-flight center, Malone has held Utah together under the

basket. Out front, Stockton has developed into the greatest assist man in league history, passing Magic Johnson in total career assists in 1995. Stockton's passes, fundamentally sound and almost always on the mark, have helped Malone become one of the highest scoring power forwards ever.

With the team up and running, Layden turned over the coaching duties to former Bulls star Jerry Sloan. With Hornecek

arriving midway through the 1993–94 season, the Jazz added yet another veteran scorer to the starting lineup. They reached the Western Conference Finals in 1994 and won a team-record 60 games in 1995 as they continue their championship quest.

Utah fell just one game shy of the NBA Finals in 1996, losing to Seattle in the conference Finals. The Jazz may sound better in New Orleans, but they look much better in Utah.

John Stockton: Taking on all-comers.

JERRY SLOAN
Master Jazzman

Ask about the crooked nose and Jerry Sloan will tell you he can't remember how many times it was broken.

"I think I broke it about seven or eight times," he says with a shrug.

Sloan made up for limited skills with determination and grit. Though just 6–5 and 200 pounds, Sloan feared no one. He directed the Bulls' defense like a general directing an army and refused to give an inch, even in practice.

He made the NBA All-Defensive First Team four times and led Chicago to a string of 50-win seasons in the early 1970s. A two-time All-Star, Sloan retired in 1975 and became a coach.

When Sloan moved into the head job with the Jazz, the team responded immediately, averaging more than 50 victories season in his first five full seasons. The Jazz also won two Midwest Division titles and 25 playoff games.

Other than Sloan's nose, there's no longer anything out of line in Utah.

Hoops Comes to Hockey Town

Head coach Brian Winters played with former NBA star center Bob Lanier and general manager Stu Jackson once coached the New York Knicks' Patrick Ewing. So it only made sense that the Grizzlies would build their first roster around a highly skilled big man. And that's exactly what Vancouver did when it made Bryant "Big Country" Reeves the team's first No. 1 draft pick.

Long before Stu Jackson became general manager of the expansion Vancouver Grizzlies he knew the job would have as much to do with education as building a franchise from the ground up.

Vancouver's sporting landscape has been dominated by hockey from its junior ranks to the professional level.

But Jackson, who coached the New York Knicks in 1989–90, thinks that's exactly why the Grizzlies popularity will explode once the NBA game arrives.

"That void could get filled here quickly," says Jackson, who has always believed in making the team and front office accessible to fans and media. "We have an opportunity, over the long term, to make the Grizzlies a focal point of people's conversations. My dream is that I'll be around here for 10 or 15 years, where I can actually hear and see that. Hockey here is what has been and will always be. But it's not true

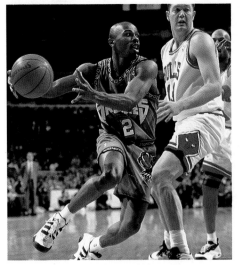

Greg Anthony leading from the front.

with this younger generation. The potential is there for a basketball explosion."

To that end, Jackson's long-term vision can be seen in the building blocks he has used to create the Grizzlies foundation.

By naming Winters, 43, as the team's first coach, Jackson chose an individual known for his ability to communicate with players. A former NBA all-star as a player, Winters learned the coaching game as an assistant under Lenny Wilkens, who has more professional coaching victories than any coach in NBA history.

"I guess one of the greatest things I've taken from him isn't even on the basketball side," says Winters, an NBA head coach for the first time. "I think as good a basketball coach as he is, Lenny is a better man. He always had his teams ready to play. As for my own style, I'd like to think I'm a teacher."

Out on the court, Jackson started building the Grizzlies roster with a combination of inside and outside toughness. In the expansion draft, Vancouver selected seasoned scorers Byron Scott, Gerald Wilkens and Blue Edwards to shore up the perimeter. Jackson then used additional expansion picks to add centers Antonio Harvey and Benoit Benjamin along with power forwards Kenny Gattison and Larry Stewart. Rodney Dent, Reggie Slater and Doug Edwards were also among the first Grizzlies.

But it was the acquisition of former Knicks point guard Greg Anthony with Vancouver's first pick in the expansion draft that made the day for Jackson and Winters.

The Grizzlies' front office felt the same way only a few days later when the 1995 NBA Draft produced 7–0 center Bryant "Big Country" Reeves and 6–5 shooting guard Lawrence Moten. Reeves, who starred at Oklahoma State, was the No. 6 choice

ROLL OF HONOR				
Conference/Division	Western/Midwest			
First NBA year	1995-96			
Home Arena details	General Motors Place (built 1995, capacity 20,004)			
Former cities/nicknames	None			
NBA Championships	None			
Playing Record	G	W	L	Pct
Regular Season	82	15	67	.183
Playoffs	None			

overall and the first ever for the Grizzlies, "Our decision to draft Bryant as our first-ever college pick reflects the premium we've placed on a big center," says Jackson. "Bryant gives us size, excellent shooting skills, solid passing, soft hands and perhaps the most important, a yeoman's work ethic."

Vancouver limped to a 15–67 record in the franchise's first season, But the fans seemed to sense that Jackson and Winters were building for the long haul. The team took a step torward building an imposing an important front line by drafting 6–10 forward Shareef Abdur-Rahim with the No. 3 pick in the 1996 NBA Draft. Abdur-Rahim's athletic shot-blocking skills should mesh with Reeve's strength to keep the Grizzlies' opponents out of the paint.

● ●

From a Distance: Bryant Reeves shoots.

BRYANT REEVES
Big Country Arrives in B.C.

Bryant Reeves is the first to admit that the thought of an NBA career wasn't even the stuff of dreams just four years ago. As an oversized but awkward country kid from Gans, Oklahoma, a small town with just over 250 people, Reeves wasn't even sure he'd have a college career much less a professional one.

"When I started college there is no way I could have even dreamed of being taken with the sixth pick in the NBA Draft," says Reeves. "It just wasn't a realistic dream for me."

But Reeves, now a 7-foot, 292-pound center, spent countless hours developing basketball skills to match his size. He worked just as tirelessly in the weight room and by the end of his sophomore season had become the first player since Wilt Chamberlain to lead the Big Eight conference in scoring and rebounding.

In his first NBA season, Reeves showed he belonged among the league's big men. Vancouver fans fell in love with their flat-topped center, and he responded by averaging 13.3 points and 7.4 rebounds.

"The guy's a miracle," says Oklahoma State coach Eddie Sutton.

Not even Reeves would argue with that.

Bullets™

Looking to Reload

Former Coach Wes Unseld was the last link to a glorious past as Washington spent years trying to reload for another attack on the Eastern Conference powers. But the rebuilding process didn't get moving for good until the Bullets found Juwan Howard in the 1994 Draft and then traded for budding superstar Chris Webber. Suddenly the Bullets are on their way back.

One way or another Chicago has usually played a key role in the success of the Bullets.

The franchise originated in 1961, in what the NBA brass considered a perfect market. Chicago had spawned the Harlem Globetrotters and some of the best college basketball of the era. But the Chicago Packers didn't come close to capturing the hearts of locals. A year later the franchise changed its name to the Zephyrs, but the impact, on and off the court, was minimal.

Though stars such as Walt Bellamy and Terry Dischinger provided a solid foundation, the team was a disaster financially and, after two years, moved to Baltimore where it assumed yet another nickname, the Bullets.

But a new location did little to improve performance until 1968. With Earl "the Pearl" Monroe operating on the outside and Wes Unseld, a muscular 245-pound center, taking care of things under the bas-

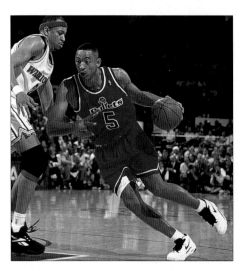

Juwan Howard makes the right moves.

ket, Baltimore won 57 games. Unseld was named Rookie of the Year and Most Valuable Player after averaging 18.2 rebounds a game.

Two years later, in 1971, the Bullets reached the NBA Finals for first time, only to be quickly eliminated by the Milwaukee Bucks. Former Boston Celtics great K.C. Jones eventually took over the coaching duties and promptly guided the Bullets back into the Finals.

With Unseld, Elvin Hayes, Phil Chenier and Mike Riordan, the Bullets knocked off Boston in the Eastern Conference Finals and met Golden State for the 1975 Championship. Now known as the Washington Bullets, following a move from Baltimore, the team won a franchise-record 60 regular-season games. But Golden State, led by superstar Rick Barry, made quick work of Washington, winning the title in four straight games.

Jones lasted one more season until management went back to Chicago for its next savior. Coach Dick Motta had turned a young Chicago Bulls franchise into an Eastern Conference power.

Within two years the Bullets were back in the NBA Finals, and this time there were no disappointments. With Hayes, Bobby Dandridge, Mitch Kupchak and Unseld, Washington had one of the most rugged frontlines in the league. The Bullets breezed through the first three rounds of the 1978 NBA Playoffs and beat Seattle in seven games for the NBA title.

Though the Bullets had a league best 54–28 record in 1978–79, the championship rematch went to the SuperSonics. That loss ended an era as Motta moved on a year later and the team faded with the retirement of Unseld and the trade of

R O L L O F H O N O R				
Conference/Division	Eastern/Atlantic			
First NBA year	1961-62			
Home Arena details	USAir Arena (built 1973, capacity 18,756)			
Former cities/nicknames	Chicago: Packers (1961-62), Zephyrs (1962-63),			
	Baltimore: Bullets (1963-73), Capital Bullets (1973-74)			
NBA Championships	1978			
Playing Record	G	W	L	Pct
Regular Season	2777	1310	1467	.472
Playoffs (Series 13-19)	163	69	94	.423

★ ★ ★ ★ ★ ★ ★ ★ ★ ★

CHRIS WEBBER
A Star Is Born

He burst onto the national scene as an 18-year-old freshman at the University of Michigan. Chris Webber, along with four other highly touted recruits, came to be known as the "Fab Five."

Webber proved ready for the NBA after just two college seasons and became the first sophomore since Magic Johnson in 1978 to be selected with the No. 1 pick in the NBA Draft when Orlando took him in 1993.

However, Golden State did just about everything to get him, trading the rights to Anfernee Hardaway and three future first-round draft picks, an enormous package, for Webber.

But Webber's relationship with coach Don Nelson soured after an often brilliant rookie season. In one of the biggest trades in years, the Warriors eventually sent Webber to Washington for Tom Gugliotta.

Only 23 years old when the 1996–97 season started, Webber stands 6–10, weighs 250 pounds and could become the league's next superstar forward.

Hayes. Since that championship, the Bullets have had just three winning seasons in 14.

Unseld returned as coach, but he was dismissed after the 1993–94 season, to be replaced as coach by Jim Lynam prior to the start of the 1994–95 season. The Bullets used the fifth pick in the 1994 Draft to select forward Juwan Howard. Then, five months later, the Bullets pulled off a dramatic trade that brought Chris Webber, Howard's former college teammate at Michigan, to Washington.

Add to Howard and Webber the size and surprising skills of 7–7 Romanian center Gheorge Muresan, plus newly acquired point guard Rod Strickland, and the Bullets don't lack for intimidation up front. For Washington, the long climb to the top of the Eastern Conference has become easier.

• •

Chris Webber (2) is the key to Washington's rise.

THE PLAYOFFS

The NBA's Second Season

For six months 29 teams battle each other for 16 precious playoff spots. The best teams jockey for home-court advantage while the up-and-coming fight each other for one of the last playoff openings. As the 82-game schedule moves toward conclusion in late April, the games become more important and the skirmishes more fierce. When it's over, eight teams from each conference embark on a second season defined by its intensity and celebrated for its opportunity. After a two-month process of elimination, only the strongest is left standing.

The goal never changes. By the time the first ball is tossed into the air in the first game of every season, NBA players and coaches already have looked down the road. For most teams, success is measured by the playoffs.

"Nothing else matters," says Chicago Bulls forward Scottie Pippen. "You can get all kinds of individual honors during the regular season, but when it comes to real accomplishment, that happens in the playoffs. That's the way it's always been for this team and I'm sure that's the way it's always been for teams that win championships."

During the 82-game war that is the regular season, teams fight each other for playoff position. For some teams, merely becoming one of the 16 teams that qualify for the postseason tournament is enough. For others, getting home-court advantage and going on to the championship round is the sole measure of success. And for a few teams like Chicago, New York and Phoenix, anything short of an NBA title represents failure.

"When I was playing, we played for championships," says former Boston Celtics guard K.C. Jones. "That's all we

thought about. We knew we'd make the playoffs. We were looking at another title."

HOW THE SYSTEM WORKS

The process, though long, is relatively simple. Eight teams from the Western Conference and eight teams from the Eastern Conference qualify for the playoffs. Regular season champions from the four divisions — Midwest, Pacific, Central and Atlantic — become the top two seeds in each conference.

The team with the best record in each conference is assured of home-court advantage through the Conference Finals. The team with the best record in the league is guaranteed home-court advantage throughout the entire playoffs.

"Home-court advantage wasn't that important to us," recalled Chicago Bulls star Michael Jordan, a three-time Finals MVP. "But for some teams that was the only way they had a chance. Winning playoff games on the road is one of the hardest things to do as a team.

Los Angeles guard Walt Hazzard fires off a pass to launch another quick break.

"Don't get me wrong. We wanted home-court advantage. Although we learned how to win on the road, we were just like every other team. We wanted to play as much as possible."

The eight teams from each conference are seeded according to their regular-season record and division finish. There are four First Round best-of-five playoff series in each conference with the No. 1 team playing the No. 8 team, the No. 2 team meeting the No. 7 team and so on.

Winners of the First Round move into the Conference Semifinals. There the series becomes best-of-seven. Once again, the team with the best regular-season record has home-court advantage, or four of the seven games on its floor.

The site of the series goes back and forth in a 2–2–1–1–1 format. In other words, the first two games are played in one city followed by two games in the other. After that the teams alternate until a winner is determined.

The Conference Finals are set up the same way as the Conference Semifinals.

The format changes slightly in the NBA Finals, where the Western Conference champion meets the Eastern Conference champ. Again, the team with the best regular-season record gets home-court advantage in the seven-game series. But this time, the series is set up in a 2–3–2 format, a change that was instituted in 1985 to lessen the burden of travel on the participants.

K.C. Jones of the Boston Celtics makes like the Leaning Tower of Pisa as the L.A. Lakers' Rudy LaRusso snags a rebound.

1980

Los Angeles vs. Philadelphia

Legendary center Kareem Abdul-Jabbar had arrived in a 1975 trade many figured would turn the Los Angeles Lakers into a dynasty. By 1979, however, it hadn't happened. Though competitive, the Lakers hadn't won a single title in the Abdul-Jabbar era. The game changed when a smiling rookie named Earvin "Magic" Johnson arrived. But was it enough to offset the brilliance of Philadelphia's Julius "Dr. J" Erving and effusive center Darryl Dawkins?

The regular season had pointed to a showdown between two of the most entertaining teams in NBA history. The Los Angeles Lakers won 60 games and rolled through the Western Conference playoff field.

Over in the East, Philadelphia reeled off 59 victories and buried Boston 4–1 in the Conference Finals.

The scene had been set. Could the Lakers, running behind 6–9 rookie guard Magic Johnson and the dominating center play of Kareem Abdul-Jabbar, fight off a 76ers attack led by Julius "Dr. J" Erving, massive center Darryl Dawkins and a deep Philadelphia roster?

By Game 6, the Lakers had proved their place. But they also needed a miracle.

They found Magic instead.

Through the first five games of the series the balance of power shifted back and forth. By Game 5, the Lakers appeared to

Trapped: Magic Johnson looks for an opening as Philadelphia's Darryl Dawkins and Julius Erving (6) close in.

have finally gained a measure of momentum, as well as a 3–2 lead in the series.

Abdul-Jabbar had been spectacular, averaging 33.4 points and 13.6 rebounds. Johnson, clearly not intimidated by his first title run, had averaged an equally impressive 17.4 points, 10.2 rebounds and 9.0 assists.

Then lightening struck. Abdul-Jabbar hobbled through the fourth quarter of Game 5 with a badly sprained left ankle. A day later, he could barely walk. As the Lakers headed to Philadelphia for Game 6, Abdul-Jabbar, the team's only real center, remained back in Los Angeles.

That's when Magic took over. Johnson moved to the center position for Game 6 and one of the most incredible individual performances in championship series history followed.

Johnson led both teams with 42 points and 15 rebounds. He was so dominant that the Lakers won by the largest margin of the series, 123–107.

A new era had dawned in Los Angeles. And it was Magic.

GAME	1980 NBA FINALS		
1	Los Angeles	109–102	Philadelphia
2	Philadelphia	107–104	Los Angeles
3	Los Angeles	111–101	Philadelphia
4	Philadelphia	105–102	Los Angeles
5	Los Angeles	108–103	Philadelphia
6	Los Angeles	123–107	Philadelphia

1984

Boston vs. Los Angeles

While Magic Johnson and Kareem Abdul-Jabbar dominated the West, Red Auerbach had done it again in the East. The Boston Celtics, one of basketball's greatest franchises, were loaded. Auerbach had drafted Larry Bird and Kevin McHale and traded for Robert Parish and Dennis Johnson. The talent extended throughout the Celtics' roster. The same, however, could be said of the Lakers. But could Boston shut down a Lakers attack now called "Showtime?"

Larry Bird and Magic Johnson had passed this way before. As college players at Indiana State and Michigan State, respectively, Bird and Johnson had led their teams into the national championship game.

But Johnson, with a much better supporting cast, stole the show. Though Bird played valiantly, he wasn't enough by himself and Michigan State won the NCAA title. When the two joined the NBA they ended up at opposite ends of the country on the league's two most storied franchises.

The rematch, however, didn't take place until 1984. The Lakers had a roster full of talent with players such as Johnson, Kareem Abdul-Jabbar, James Worthy, Byron Scott, Michael Cooper, Bob McAdoo and

Boston's Robert Parish battles the Lakers.

Jamaal Wilkes. The Celtics countered with Bird, Parish, McHale, Dennis Johnson, Quinn Buckner, Cedric Maxwell and Scott Wedman.

Through the early skirmishes and leading into Game 4, Boston appeared to be outgunned. The Lakers' fast break had produced a 2–1 advantage with Game 4 in Los Angeles.

But the Celtics refused to go quietly. By the time Game 4 ended in overtime, Boston had redirected the momentum. The Celtics had rallied from a 10-point halftime deficit and held on during a wild five-minute overtime period.

So as the Finals shifted back to Boston, so too did the Celtics' prospects for victory. Bird's brilliant 34-point, 17-rebound performance, which included 15-of-20 shooting from the floor, keyed an easy Boston victory and gave the Celtics a 3–2 lead.

Back in Los Angeles it took a furious fourth-quarter rally before the Lakers evened the series again. But Boston, playing inside fabled Boston Garden in Game 7, seemed to sense success.

Playing before another sellout in the old arena, Boston dominated. The Celtics, led by Bird and Parish, controlled the rebounds and shut down the Lakers' fast-break in a 111–102 win.

For Bird, the first rematch was his to cherish.

GAME		1984 NBA FINALS		
1	Los Angeles	115–109	Boston
2	Boston	124–121	Los Angeles (OT)
3	Los Angeles	137–104	Boston
4	Boston	129–125	Los Angeles (OT)
5	Boston	121–103	Los Angeles
6	Los Angeles	119–108	Boston
7	Boston	111–102	Los Angeles

1994

New York vs. Houston

Patrick Ewing and Hakeem Olajuwon had spent nearly a decade lifting their respective franchises toward greatness. But Olajuwon had failed in his only previous trip to the NBA Finals, while Ewing had never even had the opportunity. All that changed when they lined up opposite one another in the 1994 Finals.

GAME	1994 NBA FINALS		
1	Houston	85–78	New York
2	New York	91–83	Houston
3	Houston	93–89	New York
4	New York	91–82	Houston
5	New York	91–84	Houston
6	Houston	86–84	New York
7	Houston	90–84	New York

They had come from different parts of the world but, in June 1994, they occupied the center of professional basketball.

Patrick Ewing, born in Jamaica and raised near Boston, and Hakeem Olajuwon, the Nigerian who came to the United States to become a basketball player, became two of the most dominant big men to ever play the game. Their size, speed and remarkable quickness was always matched by fierce competitive streaks. Since they arrived in New York and Houston respectively, the twice yearly battles between Ewing and Olajuwon had almost always been special.

By the time they lined up for Game 7 of the 1994 NBA Finals, the war between the Knicks and Rockets had exacted a toll on both of them. Ewing, playing on sore knees, had been unable to find his shooting touch. In an 86–84 loss to Houston in Game 6, Ewing had hit just 6-of-20 shots in 45 grueling minutes.

"I don't care what I shoot," said Ewing, "as long as we win."

Though Olajuwon appeared fresher and at times too quick for Ewing at the offensive end, the Knicks surged behind relentless defensive pressure. The NBA's No. 1 defensive team during the regular season, New York carved out a 91–84 victory in Game 5. As the series returned to Houston, the Knicks were only a game away from their first title in 21 years.

But as it turned out, New York was close and nothing more. In Houston, the series turned toward Olajuwon. With less than 40 seconds left in Game 6, Olajuwon stole a pass and partially blocked a John Starks shot to secure Houston's slim victory and tie the series.

In Game 7, history sided with Olajuwon. The home team had won the past 19 times a playoff series had gone to Game 7, a string going back to the 1982 Eastern Conference Finals.

"I think playing for the championship transcends any history in the playoffs," insisted Riley.

History was one thing, Olajuwon, however, was quite another. Playing 46 minutes in Game 7, Olajuwon lifted the Rockets and carried them to a 90–84 victory and the franchise's first NBA Championship.

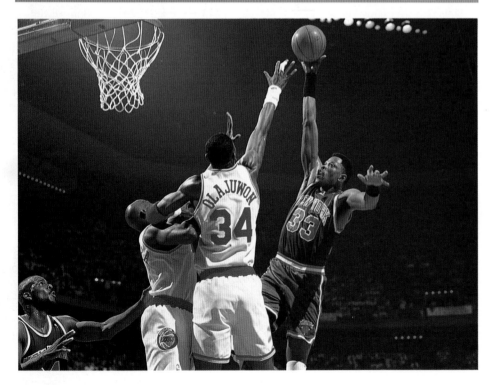

Battle of the Titans: New York's Patrick Ewing (33) hooks over Finals MVP Hakeem Olajuwon.

1995

Houston vs. Orlando

The NBA Finals once again became a battle of two big men—Houston's Hakeem Olajuwon and Orlando's Shaquille O'Neal. Not since Bill Russell and Wilt Chamberlain squared off in the 1960s had two centers of such star power matched up for the NBA title.

GAME	1995 NBA FINALS		
1	Houston	120–118	Orlando
2	Houston	117–106	Orlando
3	Houston	106–103	Orlando
4	Houston	113–101	Orlando

sweep and gave Houston a second straight title. It was the first NBA Championship in Drexler's career. As a member of the Portland Trail Blazers, Clyde the Glide had lost in two previous NBA Finals appearances.

And what of the O'Neal—Olajuwon battle in the pivot? O'Neal had a great series, averaging 28 points and 12.5 rebounds. But the crafty veteran Olajuwon outdid his younger foe, averaging 32.8 points and 11.5 rebounds while claiming his second consecutive NBA Finals MVP award.

Head to Head: Hakeem and Shaq head up in game 1.

Hakeem the Dream had led his Rockets to the 1994 NBA Championship, but many experts expected Orlando's Shaq Attack to overcome Houston's edge in experience. The Magic had the homecourt advantage and expected to get off to a fast start behind O'Neal, point guard Anfernee Hardaway and power forward Horace Grant.

However, Houston remembered that earlier in the postseason, the Magic had won the first playoff game in the franchise's history. Using experience gained in the previous year's championship run, the Rockets overcame a 20-point deficit to send Game 1 into overtime. Olajuwon tipped in a Clyde Drexler miss with just a fraction of a second left on the clock in overtime to take a 1–0 advantage.

The Rockets weren't satisfied with stealing one game on Orlando's home court. Proving that the Rockets' firepower extended beyond Olajuwon, Houston got a 31-point performance from backup guard Sam Cassell in Game 2 en route to a 117–106 victory.

The scene shifted to Houston for Games 3 and 4, but the outcome was all to familiar to the Magic. Orlando could not pound the ball inside to O'Neal often enough down the stretch of Game 3, and forward Robert Horry sank a clutch three-pointer to seal the win for Houston, 106–103.

The Magic did not give up in Game 4, but the Rockets were simply too much. Their 113–101 win sealed the

1996

Chicago vs. Seattle

• •

For just the 15th time in NBA history, the 1996 NBA Finals featured a show-down between the No. 1 and No. 2 teams in the league. Chicago, which had stormed to a record-setting 72–10 record in the regular season, was the league's top team. Seattle earned the No. 2 distinction with a 64–18.

• •

In the previous 14 No. 1—No. 2 matchups, the No. 1 team had won 11 times. The SuperSonics, fresh off back-to-back first-round playoff exits in the past two seasons, wanted to prove that they were as good as their gaudy regular-season records. Power forward Shawn Kemp and point guard Gary Payton were among the best in the league, but the Sonics and coach George Karl had little postseason success to show for it.

Meanwhile, it appeared a mere formality that Michael Jordan's Bulls would claim the title based on their amazing regular season. Once the postseason began, Jordan and forwards Scottie Pippen and Dennis Rodman sparked Chicago to an 11–1 record in the Eastern Conference playoffs.

The Bulls kept on charging as the 1996 NBA Finals started. Before the Sonics

• •

Out to Win: Michael Jordan and Dennis Rodman.

knew what had hit them, the Bulls had taken a 3–0 lead in the series behind Jordan's clutch shooting and Rodman's dominance on the boards. Kemp was a one-man show for the Sonics, but he couldn't win games by himself.

On the verge of elimination, Seattle fought back with its trademark defense, which stifled the Bulls in Games 4 and 5. The series headed back to Chicago, where the Sonics felt they had a chance to come all the way back from the 3–0 deficit.

It wasn't to be. Coach Phil Jackson motivated his Chicago troops to deliver a knockout performance on the defensive end of the court. When the buzzer sounded at the end of Game 6, the Bulls had an 87–75 victory and a fourth NBA Championship in six years.

Including the regular season and the playoffs, the Bulls had compiled an amazing 87–13 record during the 1995–96 season. After the game, Jordan—who was the MVP of the 1996 All-Star Game, regular season and NBA Finals—collapsed to the floor with relief and jubilation. After more than a year away from basketball, he had come back as a winner.

"I had a lot of things on my heart and on my mind," said Jordan, who dedicated the Game 6 win on Father's Day to his late father. "I think deep down my heart was geared to what was important to me, which is my family."

The decisive victory capped a dream season for Chicago. Aside from Jordan's impressive slew of MVP awards, the Bulls were a well-rounded team with many weapons. Jordan, Pippen and Rodman were all named to the All-Defense first team. Jackson was recognized as the NBA's Coach of the Year. For the Sonics, the loss didn't diminish their season's accomplishments. But in the end, the Bulls left no doubt as to who the NBA's No. 1 team was.

GAME	1996 NBA FINALS		
1	Chicago	107–90	Seattle
2	Chicago	92–88	Seattle
3	Chicago	108–86	Seattle
4	Seattle	107–86	Chicago
5	Seattle	89–78	Chicago
6	Chicago	87–75	Seattle

SUPERSTARS OF THE NBA

They have turned the NBA into one of the greatest shows on and off earth by combining speed, strength, style and substance. And the brightest of them are known as Superstars.

The game has always revolved around its greatest players, constantly evolving with each new talent and turning on the brilliance of each era's stars. In the early days, George Mikan dominated with a rare combination of size and skill. It was Mikan who set the stage for later star centers such as Bill Russell, Wilt Chamberlain and Kareem Abdul-Jabbar by dominating at both ends of the court.

So gifted were the early giants that rules were actually changed to keep them from twisting the entire game toward themselves. The introduction of the 24-second clock to limit offensive possession time and thus speed up the game opened the floor to another group of players. All-around stars such as Oscar Robertson showed how smaller players with multiple talents could dominate just as much as the era's big men.

But then the game took off for good on the wings of players such as Julius "Dr. J" Erving. His high-flying style and all-around brilliance created a whole new level. Dominique Wilkins, Hakeem Olajuwon, Patrick Ewing, David Robinson, and Michael Jordan, players who combined size, speed and remarkable leaping ability, became some of the game's greatest scorers. Others such as Magic Johnson and Larry Bird, with near-perfect fundamentals and an innate understanding of the game, lifted the NBA game into one of the most popular team sports in the world.

Air Jordan in mid flight against the New York Knicks.

CHARLES BARKLEY

They Call Him Sir Charles

Charles Barkley didn't look like a basketball player as a boy growing up in tiny Leeds, Alabama. His legs were heavy, his body short and wide. Coaches didn't think he was tall enough to play inside or fast enough to play guard.

So Charles went to work. He spent hours jumping back and forth over the fence behind his family's small house. By the time he entered Auburn University, Barkley's huge frame was supported by equally strong legs. Before long, nobody cared much about Barkley's relatively short stature. The Philadelphia 76ers, then one of the league's top teams with Moses Malone and Julius Erving, made Barkley the No. 5 pick in the 1984 NBA Draft.

Almost immediately Barkley, who was nicknamed "The Round Mound of Rebound," proved to be an even better player in the NBA. With the game played more freely, Barkley used his strength and speed to punish players a half foot taller. He used his bulk to hold his ground under the basket for rebounds and his lightning quick jumping ability to go up and over taller opponents.

But he could also score from anywhere on the court. In his first nine NBA seasons, Barkley never shot less than 52 per-

Call Me Sir: Charles Barkley sails in for another score.

CAREER RECORD

PERSONAL	
Birthplace/Date	Leeds, Alabama/2.20.63
Height /Weight	6-6/252
AWARDS	
MVP	1993
All-Star Selection	1987-96 (did not play 1994)
Finals MVP	None
CAREER	
University	Auburn (1981-84)
Pro. Career	12 seasons, Philadelphia 76ers (1984-92), Phoenix Suns (1992-96)

PLAYING RECORD	G	FG	Pct	FT	Pct	Reb	Ast	Stl	Bl	Pts	ppg
Regular Season	890	7,393	.549	5,502	.738	10,311	3,495	1,451	818	20,740	23.3
Playoffs	99	966	.520	682	.716	1,448	441	176	110	2,417	24.4
All-Star	8	45	.495	20	.625	60	16	12	4	113	14.1

> **"CHARLES IS A TOTALLY DOMINANT PLAYER. GUYS WHO ARE 6–4 OR 6–5 JUST AREN'T SUPPOSED TO BE ABLE TO DO THAT IN THE NBA."**
>
> Larry Bird

The Round Mound of Rebound: Barkley lives up to his nickname against the Chicago Bulls.

cent from the floor. He could hit short jump shots, long three-pointers and slam as well as any player in history.

Like Los Angeles Lakers legend Magic Johnson, Barkley also had one of the most engaging personalities in the league. Though he played with emotion that sometimes boiled over, Barkley became a favorite of fans and teammates.

"With the Sixers, even when he was new, Charles got us awake at times," says former Philadelphia guard Maurice Cheeks. "Sometimes we got on too low a flame, but then Charles would come along and slam the ball or something and we'd remember

Charles in Charge: Barkley became the Suns main man the moment he arrived in 1992.

what we were out there for. And we had better know because you didn't want Charles mad at you."

Barkley, who became known as "Sir Charles," was named to the All-NBA First Team four straight years in Philadelphia starting in 1988. In a game against New York and 7-foot center Patrick Ewing in 1987, Barkley set NBA records with 11 offensive rebounds in one quarter and 13 in one half. He also became one of the shortest players to ever lead the league in rebounding when he averaged 14.6 a game during the 1986–87 season.

But his greatest success didn't come until the 76ers shipped him to Phoenix in a blockbuster four-player trade in 1992. After performing with USA Basketball's Dream Team, Barkley turned the Suns into a title contender, leading the team to the 1993 NBA Finals. Though Phoenix lost to Michael Jordan's Chicago Bulls, Barkley earned his first Most Valuable Player award.

PATRICK EWING

New York's Tower of Power

•••

**Quiet and soft-spoken, with a gentle smile and manner,
Patrick Ewing seems nothing like the menacing shot-blocker
that he is on the basketball court.**

•••

Patrick Ewing goes up and over everyone.

atch Ewing long enough and it's hard to believe that he started playing basketball late in his youth. Watch him rally the New York Knicks past another opponent, or slap away a shot attempt, and it seems unlikely Ewing ever lacked confidence or consistency. Look over Ewing's résumé, which includes an NCAA championship at Georgetown University and Olympic gold medals in 1984 and 1992, and it's hard to think of him of anything less than the dominant big man he has become.

"Very early on, Patrick had to learn, had to be convinced, how good he really was, how good he could be," says Georgetown coach and former NBA center John Thompson. "Defensively, to help him with both his confidence and his consistency, I told him to go up and block every shot and take his chances on being called for goal-tending. The guy on the other team would remember that."

Whatever the lesson, it worked. Ewing developed into a college star at Georgetown before graduating to the New York Knicks as the first pick in the 1985 NBA Draft. Though injuries slowed Ewing in his first two NBA seasons, the marvelous

CAREER RECORD

PERSONAL											
Birthplace/Date	Kingston, Jamaica/8.5.62										
Height /Weight	7-0/240										
AWARDS											
MVP	None										
All- Star Selections	1986 (did not play, injured), 1988-95										
Finals MVP	None										
CAREER											
University	Georgetown (1981-85)										
Pro. Career	11 seasons, New York Knicks (1985-96)										

PLAYING RECORD	G	FG	Pct	FT	Pct	Reb	Ast	Stl	Bl	Pts	ppg
Regular Season	759	7,116	.520	3,832	.742	7,873	1,643	842	2,143	18,117	23.9
Playoffs	97	859	.477	454	.732	1,057	237	92	244	2,180	22.5
All-Star	9	44	.556	18	.692	60	7	11	16	106	11.8

Young and Old: Ewing teaches young Alonzo Mourning about position.

talents were obvious to everyone, partic-ularly opposing players.

Ewing was named NBA Rookie of the Year in 1986 despite missing 32 games that season. In the 1989–89 season he averaged 28.6 points while scoring from vir-tually anywhere on the court. He slammed down rim-rattling dunks, lofted soft fall away jumpers and, when teams forced him outside, dropped long-range jump shots. He also averaged nearly 11 rebounds a game and blocked a career-high 327 shots in 82 games.

Two years later, with Pat Riley taking over on the bench, Ewing's Knicks had become one of the NBA's most devastating teams. New York, led by Ewing's relentless defensive play, took the eventual champion Chicago Bulls to the Eastern Conference Finals in 1993, narrowly missing a shot at the cham-pionship round.

A year later, the Knicks came within a game of winning the 1994 NBA Championship when they fell 4–3 to Houston in the Finals.

The reason was simple: Patrick Ewing. At 7–0 and more than 240 pounds, Ewing had turned a once slender frame into a mass of muscle.

His workouts are now leg-endary around the Knicks team. As a result, Patrick Ewing has been the corner stone of the Knicks' line-up for a decade.

Strong and Agile: Ewing dunks as hard as any player in history.

"HE MADE ME FEEL LIKE AN OLD MAN IN A YOUNG MAN'S GAME WHEN HE CAME INTO THE LEAGUE. WHEN HE IS ON HIS GAME, ALL YOU CAN DO IS KEEP PUSHING HIM AND HOPE FOR THE BEST. WITH EXPERIENCE HE HAS BECOME AN AMAZING PLAYER."

Legendary center Moses Malone

ANFERNEE HARDAWAY

Lightning Strikes Twice

A year after Orlando used the No. 1 pick in the 1992 Draft to select Shaquille O'Neal, fate shined on the Magic once again. This time, however, Orlando used the No. 1 pick on Chris Webber but almost immediately traded him to Golden State for a 20-year-old guard called Penny.

No one was sure what to do until John Gabriel, the Magic's personnel director, decided he needed one more look at Anfernee Hardaway. In a quiet gym filled only with Orlando front office personnel, Hardaway put on a dazzling display of speed, quickness, stamina and leadership in a series of games with veteran players.

When the workout concluded, so too had the decision process. With O'Neal in the middle, it became clear that Hardaway was the player the Magic needed most.

Hardaway, a lean 6–7 guard, has been even better than Gabriel hoped. While his size and point guard skills draw the comparisons to Johnson, it's Hardaway's power dunks and long-range shooting ability that make him unique. Tree Rollins, Orlando's veteran back-up center, remembers one slam in particular over New York's Patrick Ewing that left everyone rubbing their eyes.

"Patrick is seven feet and about 250 pounds, and Penny is 6–7 and skinny as a rail," says Rollins. "When Penny took off

Anfernee Hardaway passes as well as he scores.

CAREER RECORD											
PERSONAL											
Birthplace/Date	Memphis, Tennessee/7.16.72										
Height /Weight	6-7/200										
AWARDS											
MVP	None										
All-Star Selection	1995										
Finals MVP	None										
CAREER											
University	Memphis (1990-93)										
Pro. Career	3 seasons, Orlando Magic (1993-96)										
PLAYING RECORD	G	FG	Pct	FT	Pct	Reb	Ast	Stl	Bl	Pts	ppg
Regular Season	241	1,258	.494	1,046	.762	1,129	1,677	486	118	4,706	19.5
Playoffs	36	267	.467	149	.749	155	255	65	22	748	20.8*
All-Star	2	10	.588	8	.800	8	18	2	0	30	15.0

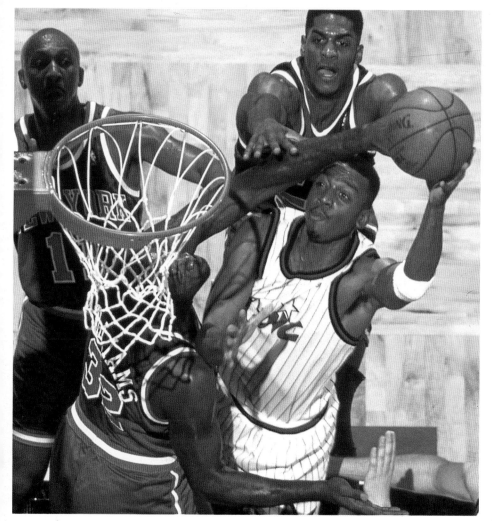

Three New York defenders can't stop Hardaway.

Seattle's All-Star guard Gary Payton described Hardaway in five words: "Best guard in the NBA."

Hardaway is not sure the label fits just yet. But does admit to a fondness for the kind of plays that bring fans to their feet.

"I like to entertain," he says. "Most of all, I want to win, but when I do something special, I can feel the vibe from the crowd. I live for the *ooh*, the *aah*."

Penny truly proved his worth during the 1995–96 season. A broken thumb sidelined Shaq for nearly 30 games. In his absence, Hardaway raised his game another notch and helped the Magic get off to a fast start.

Only the eventual NBA Champion Chicago Bulls could keep Orlando from another Finals appearance.

One thing is for sure: Anfernee Hardaway has arrived as a superstar.

Hardaway slams the Washington Bullets.

"PICKING A FAVORITE PENNY HARDAWAY PLAY IS LIKE PICKING OUT WHICH ONE OF THE STARS UP IN THE SKY SHINES THE BRIGHTEST. THERE'S SO MANY OF 'EM, YOU JUST CAN'T PICK ONE."

Larry Finch, University of Memphis head coach

for the hoop, I thought Patrick would either get the block or flatten him. But Penny just exploded to the basket, and, *wham!* It was over."

In an often spectacular rookie season in 1993–94, Hardaway averaged 16.0 points, 6.6 assists, 5.4 rebounds and more than two steals a game. And in the playoffs, the first postseason test for the young Orlando franchise, Hardaway produced better numbers in virtually every statistical category.

More importantly, the Magic improved dramatically, winning a franchise record 50 games. By the start of the 1994–95 season, Hardaway was considered the league's next great guard and Orlando was suddenly a genuine championship contender.

The Magic improved when O'Neal arrived. But Orlando didn't take that next step forward until Hardaway came aboard.

In 1994–95, with the addition of former Chicago forward Horace Grant, the Magic finished with the best record in the Eastern Conference and made it all the way through to the NBA Finals, where the Houston Rockets swept Orlando.

GRANT HILL
The Key to Detroit's Future

The comparisons started the moment Grant Hill threw down his first thundering dunk. With a long, slender body and enough skills to play four positions, Hill recalled some of the league's brightest stars.

The quick first step reminded some of Michael Jordan. Others saw Scottie Pippen in Hill's unusual combination of talents. Indeed, Hill proved immediately that he belonged amid the NBA elite on and off the court. Intelligent, cool and mature beyond his years, Hill did look a lot like Jordan during his first winter in Detroit.

The Pistons, looking for another star after Isiah Thomas retired, wanted only one player in the 1994 NBA Draft. Though they had the third pick, Detroit

Grant Hill: Memories of a young Michael Jordan

worked feverishly to move up.

"I wanted Grant Hill," said Billy McKinney, then the vice president of operations. "We all did. But we were afraid someone else would take him before the third pick."

It didn't happen. Hill, who played on back-to-back NCAA Championship teams at Duke, went to the Pistons and before he played a single NBA game, he had fielded endorsement calls from some of the world's largest corporations. However rare his athletic gifts, Hill's personality was even more unique.

"He's a special person," said Don

CAREER RECORD

PERSONAL											
Birthplace/Date	Dallas, Texas/10.5.72										
Height /Weight	6-8/225										
AWARDS											
MVP	None										
All Star Selection	1995										
Finals MVP	None										
CAREER											
University	Duke (1990–1994)										
Pro. Career	2 seasons, Detroit Pistons (1994-96),										

PLAYING RECORD	G	FG	Pct	FT	Pct	Reb	Ast	Stl	Bl	Pts	ppg
Regular Season	150	1,072	.469	859	.742	1,228	901	228	110	3,012	20.1
Playoffs	36	267	.467	149	.749	155	255	65	22	748	20.8
All-Star	2	10	.588	8	.800	8	18	2	0	30	15.0

> **"I ALWAYS FELT HE WOULD BE THE NEXT IMPACT PLAYER IN THE LEAGUE. I THINK HE'S IN A CLASS BY HIMSELF."**
>
> Former Charlotte Coach Allan Bristow

Hill (left) reaches over Nick Van Exel trying to steal the ball.

Chaney, the Pistons' coach in Hill's rookie season, "not only in the way he plays, but how he handles himself. His parents did a great job instilling values in him."

Grant Hill grew up in the shadow of a famous father, Calvin, who starred as an NFL runningback. Refusing to expose his son to the brutality of his profession, Calvin guided Grant toward soccer. And for much of his early athletic life, Grant thought that was to be his game. At least until he started to grow. Before long, soccer had been eclipsed by basketball and college coaches were knocking at his door.

"It just seems like yesterday I was in high school," he says, "pretending I was Julius Erving and pretending I was Isiah Thomas and pretending I was Michael Jordan. Every time I stepped on the court, I was somebody else. Now, in some way I'm kind of in their shoes, in the sense that people do the same with me — I guess. So I'm told. It's just hard to believe."

These days, nothing about Hill surprises anyone but himself. He not only got off to a brilliant start in his first season, but Hill became the first rookie to ever lead the fan voting for the All-Star Game.

Hill repeated as top vote-getter in his second year and became a nightly threat to record a triple-double. Spurred by Hill's consistently remarkable play, the Pistons made the playoffs for the first time in three years.

With Hill at the helm, the Pistons should be making postseason plans for many years to come.

MAGIC JOHNSON

Basketball's True Magician

Few nicknames in NBA history have been more fitting than the one hung on Earvin Johnson.

Johnson was only a high school player when a local sportswriter noticed the remarkable ballhandling and passing skills. "Magic," thought the writer. Indeed, it often looked as if Johnson's wizardry could be nothing else.

By the time he left Michigan State University after just two seasons, one of the greatest rivalries in NBA history had been set. Johnson's Michigan State team defeated Larry Bird's Indiana State University squad for the 1979 NCAA championship. A year later, Johnson had landed with the Los Angeles Lakers and Bird with the Boston Celtics.

The two would go head-to-head for an entire decade, with Johnson leading the Lakers to five NBA Championships, two of those against Bird's Celtics.

Johnson showed the world just how dominant a 6–9 guard can be when he took over at center in Game 6 of the 1980 NBA Finals. With Kareem Abdul-Jabbar injured and unable to play, Johnson played opposite Philadelphia's Darryl Dawkins. Johnson dominated the game by scoring 42 points while the Lakers rolled to their first championship of the Magic era.

Another Magic Show: Johnson rises up and over the defense.

CAREER RECORD

PERSONAL											
Birthplace/Date	Lansing, Michigan/8.14.59										
Height /Weight	6-9/225										
AWARDS											
MVP	1987, 1989, 1990										
All-Star Selections	1980, 1982-92 (did not play 1989, injured)										
Finals MVP	1980, 1982, 1987										
CAREER											
University	Michigan State (1977-79)										
Pro. Career	13 seasons, Los Angeles Lakers (1979-91, 96)										

PLAYING RECORD	G	FG	Pct	FT	Pct	Reb	Ast	Stl	Bl	Pts	ppg
Regular Season	906	6,211	.520	4,960	.848	6,559	10,141	1,724	374	17,707	19.5
Playoffs	190	1,291	.506	1,068	.838	2,896	2,340	358	64	3,701	19.5
All-Star	11	64	.489	38	.905	57	127	21	7	191	16.0

The Eyes Have It: With remarkable court vision and a stunning ability to find openings, Johnson became one of the greatest passers in history.

He would go on to win three Most Valuable Player awards and make the All-NBA First Team nine straight years starting in 1983. But it was Johnson's exuberance and dazzling play making that led writers to name the Lakers attack "Showtime."

Magic returned, older and stronger, for a brief comeback during the 1995–96 season. Playing both point guard and power forward, the older and wiser Johnson led the Lakers into the playoffs. Even though the Lakers lost in the first round to Houston, younger fans had the chance to see Magic do what he does best.

"He wanted the fans and his teammates to enjoy every success on the court, says Abdul-Jabbar, a teammate for 10 years. "The quintessential Earvin experience didn't start until he passed his man and started for an easy layup. Then, just as he had to deal with a last second attempt to block his shot, the Magic Show would really begin. Doing what he did under the pressure of competition was one of the greatest continuous athletic feats ever."

Johnson's infectious smile and easy-going personality made him a one-man show on or off the court.

"Before Michael Jordan," says Larry Bird, "Magic was the only player that I'd pay money to see. He always played the game the way I thought it should be played."

"When he came to the Lakers it was like a brand new product," said former Lakers Coach Pat Riley. "Nobody knew what was going on. Then, bam! Six trips to the Finals in eight years. He's probably the greatest team showman the game has ever seen."

Such was the magic of Earvin Johnson.

"MAGIC RAN THE GAME LIKE A DISC JOCKEY RUNNING A DISCO."

Kareem Abdul-Jabbar, Johnson's teammate for 10 years

MICHAEL JORDAN

Rare Air

• •

According to Michael Jordan, it all started with "The Shot."

• •

Just a freshman at the University of North Carolina, Jordan hit the first game-winning shot of what would become an illustrious career. With the clock winding down, Jordan drained a medium-range jump shot that propelled North Carolina to the national championship and a 63–62 victory over rival Georgetown.

"That's where I think my career really began," says Jordan. "I proved to myself that I could deliver in a pressure situation."

And Jordan never stopped delivering. He led the U.S. men's basketball team to the Gold Medal in 1984 Los Angeles Olympics before starting an often amazing professional

Look Out Below: Air Jordan lifts off against Philadelphia.

career in Chicago. After leading the Bulls to three consecutive championships he stunned the basketball world in 1993 by announcing his retirement from the game.

Then, after briefly playing professional baseball in the Chicago White Sox system, Jordan returned to the NBA in 1995 with just over a month left in the regular season and led a revived Bulls team into the NBA Playoffs once again.

Jordan averaged 28.2 points while leading the team in rebounds, assists and steals and was named NBA Rookie of the Year in 1985. Ironically, it was Jordan's second season that left a lasting impression. After missing 64 regular season games with a broken foot, Jordan returned in time for the playoffs against the eventual champion Boston Celtics.

Jordan scored 49 points in Game 1 at

CAREER RECORD

PERSONAL											
Birthplace/Date	Brooklyn, NY/2.17.63										
Height /Weight	6-6/198										
AWARDS											
MVP	1988, 1991, 1992, 1996										
All-Star Selections	1985-93 (did not play 1986, injured), 1996										
Finals MVP	1991, 1992, 1993, 1996										
CAREER											
University	North Carolina (1981-84)										
Pro. Career	11 seasons, Chicago Bulls (1984-93, 1995-96)										
PLAYING RECORD	G	FG	Pct	FT	Pct	Reb	Ast	Stl	Bl	Pts	ppg
Regular Season	766	9,161	.512	5,733	.844	4,879	4,377	2,025	739	24,489	32.0
Playoffs	139	1,718	.495	1,159	.831	895	857	314	129	4,717	33.9
All-Star	9	82	.509	31	.775	35	1	1	6	197	21.9

Boston and then, in perhaps the greatest Playoff performance of all time, bombed Celtics' defensive whiz Dennis Johnson for 63 points in Game 2. It took two overtimes before the heavily favored Celtics eventually ended the Bulls charge.

"He just flat out came down and let us know what he was going to do and for the most part, he did it," said Boston superstar Larry Bird later. "He was a completely different player from anything I've seen. He's literally on a different level."

Jordan won seven straight scoring titles, matching Wilt Chamberlain's record, and became the league's best defensive guard.

In one of the most remarkable individual seasons in league history, Jordan was named Most Valuable Player and Defensive Player of the Year while leading the league in scoring and steals during the 1987–88 season. He also won his second Nestlé Slam-Dunk Championship.

With a competitive streak that amazed even his coaches, Jordan often left his opponents stunned and fans standing in amazement.

Jordan's performances were so electrifying that his popularity actually transcended the sport. Thanks to the "Air Jordan" line, Nike became the world's biggest athletic shoe company. Thanks to his personality, Jordan's endorsement deals generated as much as $30 million a year.

On the court, Jordan carried Chicago to three consecutive championships. He also became the first player to be named MVP in three straight NBA Finals.

One season after his comeback, Jordan once again reached the pinnacle of professional basketball. He led the Bulls to an NBA-record 72–10 record with another MVP season, which included another All-Defense team selection and MVP honors in the NBA All-Star Game. In the playoffs, Chicago bulldozed the SuperSonics to win a fourth title in six seasons. Again, Jordan was the MVP of the Finals and the greatest player in basketball history had pulled off one of the greatest comebacks in the history of sports.

. . . .

"MAYBE IT'S GOD DISGUISED AS MICHAEL JORDAN."

Larry Bird

. . . .

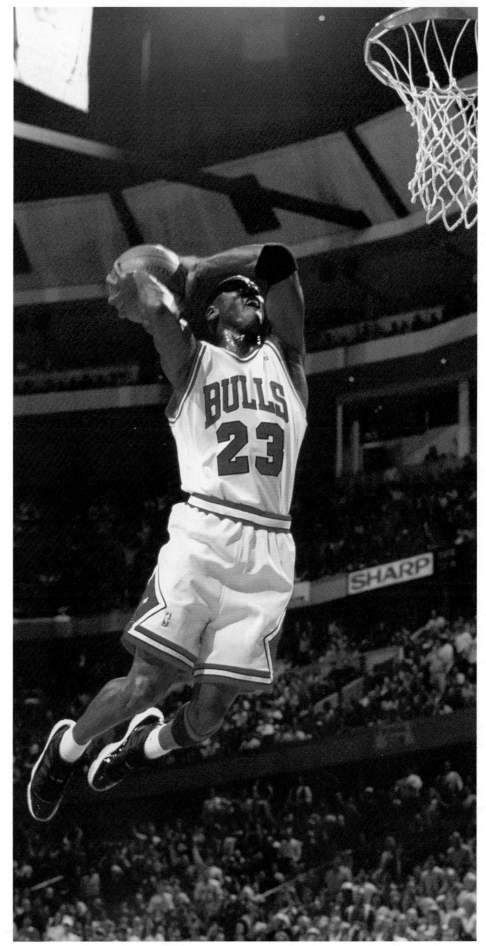

SHAWN KEMP
A SuperSonic Star in the Making

Just 19 years old, Shawn Kemp hadn't played a minute of college basketball in the year since he left high school when the Seattle SuperSonics called. A brilliant player throughout his youth, Kemp's 6–10 frame was as agile and quick as those of players six inches shorter.

So when he enrolled at the University of Kentucky, coaches there thought Kemp could develop into one of the greatest college players in history. But a dispute ended Kemp's stay quickly and suddenly he was without a team and to some extent, a future as well. He transferred to a junior college and sat out the basketball season.

On the playgrounds, Kemp was a legend. According to a friend, Kemp once dunked so hard on an outdoor rim that "sparks flew off" as the ball blew through. NBA executives had heard these stories too.

But when Kemp entered the 1989 Draft

Sonic Boomers: Shawn Kemp and Gary Payton in the 1996 NBA Finals

without a single year of college basketball behind him, the skeptics shook their head. Although Moses Malone, Darryl Dawkins and Bill Willoughby had gone from high school directly into the pros, times had changed. No player, especially one as unpolished as Kemp, could make the transition these days.

Seattle thought otherwise. The SuperSonics selected Kemp with the 17th pick overall in 1989. Kemp quickly proved the doubters wrong. He could dunk as well as any player in the league, his jumping ability stunning for a man his size. He also blocked shots with a vengeance.

In his second NBA season, Kemp aver-

CAREER RECORD

PERSONAL

Birthplace/Date	Elkhart, Indiana/11.26.69
Height /Weight	6-10/245

AWARDS

MVP	None
All-Star selections	1993-96
Finals MVP	None

CAREER

University	Trinity Junior College (did not play – left school before season)
Pro. Career	7 seasons, Seattle SuperSonics (1989-96)

PLAYING RECORD	G	FG	Pct	FT	Pct	Reb	Ast	Stl	Bl	Pts	ppg
Regular Season	544	3,146	.522	2,328	.728	5,171	940	650	878	8,632	15.9
Playoffs	62	386	.509	354	.787	641	117	79	117	1,127	18.2
All-Star	4	13	.419	6	.750	20	7	1	4	32	8.0

aged 15.0 points and 8.4 rebounds. He also had become the foundation for a SuperSonics team on the rise.

"The thing that Shawn has had going for him all along with his skills is his love for the game and his work ethic," says former Seattle coach K.C. Jones. "That's at the core of what is making him a great player.

"The only thing that ever really concerned me as far as his quick move into the pros was how he would react to the way that the fans react to NBA-style player. A part of you must become a performer as much as a player and you could see that he was a little slow to become accustomed to the oohs and aahs of the fans at his spectacular play."

Kemp became one of the most dynamic one-man shows in basketball with a dazzling array of dunks and slams. But he also developed into a complete player, propelling the SuperSonics into the 1993 Western Conference Finals. For Kemp, that season represented his coming out party as one of the league's developing superstars.

Kemp was a member of USA Basketball's 1994 team that won the World Championships of Basketball in Canada.

"Shawn," says teammate Nate McMillan, "has become the elite player we have been waiting for."

Kemp finally led the Sonics past previous playoff disasters with a dominant performance. The one-time "Man-Child" was simply The Man as only the Bulls, propelled by the great Michael Jordan, could keep the Sonics from an NBA title. While he lost in his first trip to the NBA Finals, Kemp had won the respect of basketball fans everywhere.

· ·

"SHAWN HAS THAT GREAT COMBINATION OF SKILL AND CREATIVITY. HE IS VERY SIMILAR TO THE WAY I WAS WHEN I WAS YOUNGER."

Michael Jordan

· ·

Shawn Kemp aiming to add to his impressive points total

KARL MALONE

This Mailman Delivers

Off the court, Karl Malone doesn't look much like a professional basketball player.

During the summer he operates an 18-wheel custom-made truck that hauls a variety of products to stores throughout the West. He owns a ranch in Louisiana, usually drives a pick-up truck to Utah Jazz games and would rather wear a 10-gallon hat and cowboy boots than gold chains and Gucci loafers.

But once on the court, Malone plays like a man possessed. When he isn't operating his trucking company or overseeing his ranch, Malone spends his summers lifting weights and fine-tuning his body. And no one knows that more than opposing power forwards. Not only is Malone one of the strongest players in the league, but at 6–9 and 256-pounds, he might be one of the best conditioned athletes on the planet.

"The guy is relentless," says former NBA center Dave Corzine. "He never stops working. It's almost as if he gets stronger as the game goes on. He's a machine."

Utah drafted Malone out of Louisiana Tech University, a small school tucked deep into the Louisiana countryside. Nicknamed "The Mailman" because, according to supporters, "he always delivered," Malone went to work on his game. A poor free-throw shooter as a rookie, Malone was hitting more than 70 percent two years later. An average scorer at first, Malone became the highest scoring power forward in the NBA. A sometimes disinterested defensive player, Malone became one of

Calm Delivery: Malone lifts off for another two points.

CAREER RECORD

PERSONAL											
Birthplace/Date	Summerfield, Louisiana/7.24.63										
Height /Weight	6-9/256										
AWARDS											
MVP	None										
All- Star Selections	1988-96 (did not play 1990, injured)										
Finals MVP	None										
CAREER											
University	Louisiana Tech (1981-85)										
Pro. Career	11 seasons, Utah Jazz (1985-96)										

PLAYING RECORD	G	FG	Pct	FT	Pct	Reb	Ast	Stl	Bl	Pts	ppg
Regular Season	898	8,648	.525	5,984	.726	9,733	2,819	1,304	756	23,343	26.0
Playoffs	97	958	.475	728	.725	1,111	275	147	74	2,646	27.3
All-Star	7	48	.558	26	.722	63	16	8	4	122	17.4

Conference All-Star team every year since 1988.

"There's only one way I know how to play the game," says Malone, "and that's all out. If you're not going to go at it like I do, then find someplace else to play."

"IF YOU DON'T COME READY TO PLAY, KARL WILL CHEW YOU UP AND SPIT YOU OUT,"

Former NBA center Dave Corzine

the best end-to-end players in the game.

And despite playing perhaps the toughest position in the league, Malone missed just four games his first nine seasons. That's one reason Malone has been a member of the All-NBA First Team for seven consecutive years going into the 1995–96 season. He also was a member of USA Basketball's Dream Team in 1992 and 1996 and had led the Jazz in scoring and rebounding for eight straight seasons.

"They don't come any tougher than Karl," says former Chicago Bull John Paxson. "He runs the court like a guard, blocks shots like a center and rebounds like no one I've ever seen. There really isn't anything he can't do which is scary for someone as big as he is."

Few players have ever done as much at both ends of the court as Malone. He hasn't averaged less than 25.2 points a game since his second season. Overall, Malone has averaged an astounding 26.0 points and 10.8 rebounds since he entered the league. Which is exactly why Malone has been a member of the Western

Jazz Man: As strong as any player in the league and driven to succeed, Malone takes control at both ends of the court. Top Karl comes up with some magic tricks of his own.

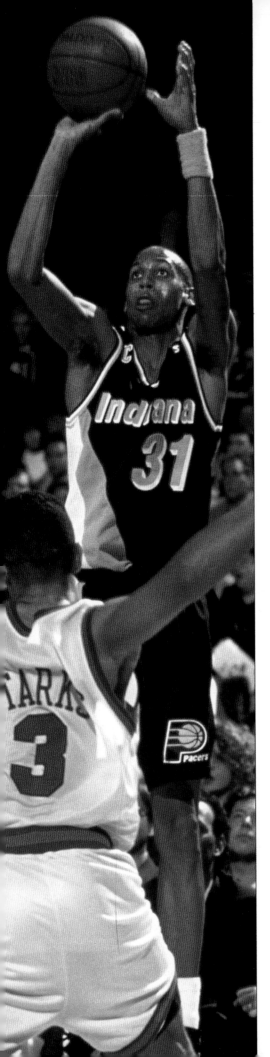

REGGIE MILLER

Long-Range Bomber

The noise never bothered Reggie Miller. He had heard the booming voices of those trying to throw off his concentration from the moment he startled tossing shots toward a backyard basket.

First his brothers, then his sister, Cheryl, perhaps the most famous female basketball player ever, would hound Reggie as he attempted to compete in the often intense family basketball games. Later, as Miller grew into one of southern California's greatest high school players, opponents would chant a sarcastic "Cheryl" whenever Reggie went up for a shot.

Miller, a slender 6–7 shooting guard with remarkable range, heard all the noise but he learned not to listen. His concentration, particularly at the free throw line, became legendary. And during games, no matter how early or late, Miller's jump shot rarely faltered.

So when New York fan Spike Lee screamed at Miller during Game 5 of Indiana's 1994 Eastern Conference Finals series against the Knicks, Miller simply turned up the volume. In one of the great individual performances in playoff history, Miller bombed the Knicks for 25 fourth-quarter points and carried the Pacers to a stunning 93-86 victory at Madison Square Garden.

Reggie Miller's jump shot is one the NBA's best.

CAREER RECORD

PERSONAL											
Birthplace/Date	Riverside, California/8.24.65										
Height /Weight	6-7/185										
AWARDS											
MVP	None										
All-Star Selection	1990, 1995, 1996										
Finals MVP	None										
CAREER											
University	UCLA (1983-87)										
Pro. Career	9 seasons, Indiana Pacers (1987-96)										

PLAYING RECORD	G	FG	Pct	FT	Pct	Reb	Ast	Stl	Bl	Pts	ppg
Regular Season	720	4,627	.491	3,188	.878	2,270	2,320	884	184	14,073	19.6
Playoffs	49	385	.481	322	.861	157	128	55	10	1,211	24.7
All-Star	3	9	.450	0		3	7	3	1	21	7.0

"I always had the ability to tune things out," says Miller. "And that's exactly what I did in that fourth quarter. It's almost a natural thing for me, a reflex. You have to have gone through it to get used to it. Everyone in this league knows how to play or they wouldn't be here. But the best players, guys like Michael Jordan and Larry Bird, were also great mentally. That's what it takes."

For Miller, the mental gymnastics started early. He developed his high, arching jump shots during pick up games with his brothers or one-on-one tangles with Cheryl. The form, almost from the outset, was virtually perfect.

Despite shooting mainly from the outside, Miller never hit less than 50.9 percent during four years at UCLA. Through his first seven NBA seasons, Miller shot 49.8 percent from the floor with nearly 30 percent of all field goal attempts from beyond the three-point line. In his first season, Miller broke Larry Bird's rookie record for three-pointers. At the free throw line Miller has established himself as one of the greatest shooters in history with an 87.7 percent career mark.

All of which is even more remarkable given Miller's early years. For most of his first five years, Miller's legs were supported by braces. Doctors warned Reggie's parents that their son might never be able to run and play like the other kids. In the Miller household, however, those kind of negative thoughts were not accepted.

"It's all in the mind," says Miller. "That's what separates the good players from the great ones."

"I LIKE PLAYING HARD. I'LL GIVE 110 PERCENT EVERY TIME I GO ON THE FLOOR AND I'LL DO WHATEVER IT TAKES FOR MY TEAM TO WIN."
Reggie Miller

Untouchable: Miller (right) swerves past New York's John Starks.

ALONZO MOURING

Seriously Hot

The scowl that routinely forms on the face of Alonzo Mourning is designed to send a messasge. Sensitive and caring off the court, Mourning wants teammates and opponents alike to know he's serious about taking the Heat to an NBA Championship.

At first, no one knew what to make of the furrowed brow and menacing scowl. He had been a star at Georgetown University and worked out with New York Knicks center Patrick Ewing, himself a Georgetown graduate, in the summer. Ewing's cold efficiency made an impression, but Mourning's own burning desire fueled his approach.

From the moment he arrived in Charlotte, the 6–10 center made his inten-

Alonzo Mourning warming up for the Heat.

tions clear to all those around him. Bump Mourning under the basket and he'll bump right back. It didn't matter whether the loose elbow came from. Mourning never gave an inch.

"It's my intensity level on the floor," says Mourning, who played in his first All-Star Game in 1994. "People think I'm an angry player, but my expression is a different zone. I'm trying to focus what I have to do on the floor. If I played against someone who was smiling all the time, I wouldn't take him seriously. I want people

CAREER RECORD

PERSONAL											
Birthplace/Date	Chesapeake, Virgiana/2.8.70										
Height /Weight	6-10/240										
AWARDS											
MVP	None										
All Star Selection	1994-95 (did not play 1994, injured)										
Finals MVP	None										
CAREER											
University	Georgetown (198-92)										
Pro. Career	4 seasons, Charlotte Hornets (1992-95), Miami Heat (1995-96)										

PLAYING RECORD	G	FG	Pct	FT	Pct	Reb	Ast	Stl	Bl	Pts	ppg
Regular Season	285	2,133	.515	1,906	.745	2,903	432	173	873	6,192	21.7
Playoffs	16	112	.467	128	.780	160	28	11	47	356	22.3
All-Star	2	5	.333	2	.667	9	1	0	2	12	6.0

to take me seriously. I'm out there trying not to make a mistake, trying to work as hard as I can for my team. I can't control perceptions. But I think my game thrives off intensity."

And that's enough for the Hornets. Charlotte improved from 31 victories to 44 and the franchise's first playoff berth in Mourning's first season (1992–93). But it was during the 1993 Playoffs that Mourning proved just how much he means to the Hornets franchise and just how good he might yet become.

Mourning's often brilliant rookie season included three victories against Shaquille O'Neal's Orlando Magic. Though smaller than all of the league's premier centers, Mourning never allowed size to become an issue. Indeed, Mourning seemed to relish the role as underdog.

No one was that more apparent than Charlotte's grueling five-game match with New York in the 1993 Eastern Conference Semifinals. Though the Knicks came away with a 4–1 decision in the best-of-7 series, New York needed every minute of every game to get the job done.

Matched against Ewing in the middle, Mourning played him nearly even. When the Hornets first postseason ended, Mourning had averaged 23.8 points, nearly 10 rebounds and more than three blocked shots through nine playoff games opposite veteran centers Robert Parish and Ewing.

The 1995–96 season saw Mourning move to Miami in a blockbuster trade. Teamed with coach Pat Riley, Mourning became a dominant force for the Heat, using his determination to rally his new team to a playoff berth. Miami fans have quickly become accustomed to Mourning turning up the Heat on both offense and defense.

"ALONZO'S ONE OF THE TOUGHEST GUYS IN THE LEAGUE. HE'S THE TASMANIAN DEVIL, ALL WHIRLS, TWIRLS AND TURNS."
Detroit assistant coach John Bach

Mourning gets the job done, this time against the Bulls' Dennis Rodman.

HAKEEM OLAJUWON

The Dream Comes True

For most of his youth, Hakeem Olajuwon figured he'd be a soccer player. No one played basketball much in Lagos, Nigeria, while he was growing up, so he became the goalkeeper on a soccer team.

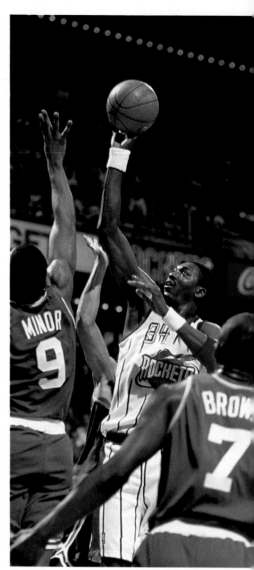

Hakeem pushes one over the Celtics.

Nowadays Olajuwon, who changed his name from Akeem to Hakeem in 1991, credits the defensive skills he learned playing soccer with helping make him a defensive giant in the NBA. Then again, the fact Olajuwon even made it to America, much less the greatest basketball league in the world, once seemed like a longshot.

He arrived at the University of Houston in 1980 with only basic basketball skills, but daunting physical gifts. Standing 7 feet tall and able to move like a smaller man,

Olajuwon caught onto the game quickly thanks to summer workouts with NBA star Moses Malone.

After just three college seasons, he had become a dominant player capable of turning an entire game around almost entirely by himself.

With the No. 1 pick in the 1984 Draft, the Houston Rockets merely looked across town to find their savior. Olajuwon, who had improved dramatically during college, developed even faster in the NBA, leading the league in offensive rebounds and aver-

aging 20.6 points and 11.9 rebounds.

Olajuwon and 7–4 Ralph Sampson became known as the "Twin Towers" and Houston became one of the league's forces. In just two seasons, the Rockets went from 29 victories and one of the league's worst records, to the 1986 NBA Finals against Larry Bird's Boston Celtics. Just as quickly, Olajuwon became a dominant center with a variety of defensive and offensive skills.

"I never felt anyone could play Hakeem one-on-one," says former NBA coach and player K.C. Jones. "To defense him you either had to deny him the ball, or bump him, and collapse players around him to force him to give up the ball."

"When he's on, which is most of the time, Hakeem is unstoppable," says Miami Heat coach Pat Riley. "We always told our defenders, 'Don't let him touch the ball.'"

By the time Olajuwon did touch the ball

CAREER RECORD

PERSONAL											
Birthplace/Date	Lagos, Nigeria/1.21.63										
Height /Weight	7-0/255										
AWARDS											
MVP	1994, 1995										
All-Star selections	1985-90, 1992-96										
Finals MVP	1994, 1995										
CAREER											
University	Houston (1980-84)										
Pro. Career	12 seasons, Houston Rockets (1984-96)										
PLAYING RECORD	G	FG	Pct	FT	Pct	Reb	Ast	Stl	Bl	Pts	ppg
Regular Season	900	8,673	.516	4,478	.711	11,023	2,393	1,694	3,190	21,840	24.3
Playoffs	115	1283	.530	632	.716	1,345	388	195	408	3,202	27.8
All-Star	11	40	.392	25	.521	91	16	15	22	102	9.6

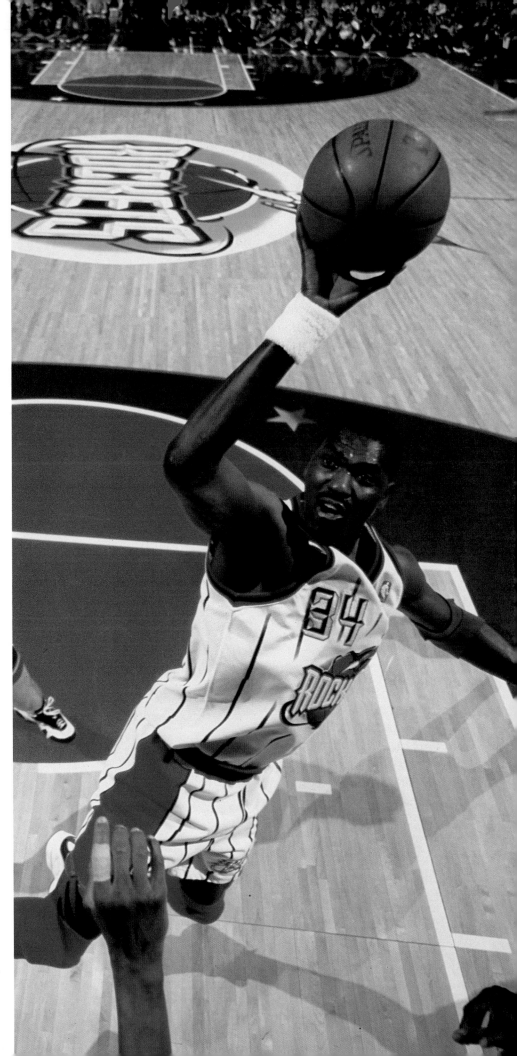

Olajuwon's ballhandling skills have helped him develop into one of the best all-around centers ever to play the game.

it was usually too late to do anything but hope he missed. His spin moves to the basket often leave defenders stuck in their tracks. His ability to get into the air quickly makes him capable of dunking anything in close to the basket. But it's Olajuwon's fadeaway jump shot, like Kareem Abdul-Jabbar's sky hook, that has become the most unstoppable shot in the league.

"Hakeem is unstoppable. There's no defense anyone can devise to prevent him from doing whatever," says Magic Johnson of Olajuwon. "He controls every game he's in. He can score inside. He runs the break. He has impeccable footwork. He is the essence of a complete player." Olajuwon developed into a complete player in the course of several seasons. In the same time, he developed into a team player. He raised his assists total to get his teammates more involved. But Olajuwon is still able to take over a game and win it for the Rockets.

And it was Olajuwon who carried the Rockets to a dramatic Game 7 victory over New York in the 1994 NBA Finals for Houston's first championship.

Despite battling anaemia toward the end of the 1994–95 regular season, Olajuwon led Houston not only into the playoffs but also to a second straight NBA Championship and his second personal NBA Finals MVP award, becoming only the second player—after Michael Jordan—to win the award in consecutive seasons.

"Olajuwon is blessed with grace, ability and quickness," says former NBA superstar Rick Barry. "To a large extent, his edge is his ability to beat his opponents physically. He also outworks them. His relentlessness, his second and third jumps on the offensive glass, is unparalleled in the NBA." That's why he's now known as "The Dream."

"IN TERMS OF RAW ATHLETIC ABILITY, HAKEEM IS THE BEST I HAVE EVER SEEN."

Magic Johnson

SHAQUILLE O'NEAL
The Shaq Attack

The stories preceded Shaquille O'Neal.

More than once during his dramatic college career at Louisiana State University, O'Neal tore a basket clean off the backboard while executing a dunk. His strength and size reminded some of Wilt Chamberlain. His ability to block shots recalled the Bill Russell era. Some wondered if O'Neal might be the best of both of them, a huge player with the athletic ability to lift an entire team.

O'Neal arrived in Orlando following the 1992 Draft, and coaches and players were still wondering just how good the 7–1, 301-pound center might become.

He was just 20 years old when the Magic played its first game with him in the middle. And no one, not even veteran centers such as Patrick Ewing, David Robinson and Hakeem Olajuwon, seemed to make much of an impression on O'Neal. Instead of feeling his way through the league, O'Neal attacked.

He averaged 23.4 points despite constant double-teams and grabbed an impressive 13.8 rebounds a game. He also blocked shots, 286 of them in his first 81 professional games to become the easy choice as NBA Rookie of the Year.

"Shaq is much more athletic than I ever thought he would be," says former Orlando coach Matt Guokas. "I played

There is nothing magical about this Shaq Attack.

CAREER RECORD

PERSONAL

Birthplace/Date	Newark, NJ/3.6.72
Height /Weight	7-1/301

AWARDS

MVP	None
All- Star Selections	1993-96
Finals MVP	None

CAREER

University	Louisiana State (1989-92)
Pro. Career	4 seasons, Orlando Magic (1992-96)

PLAYING RECORD	G	FG	Pct	FT	Pct	Reb	Ast	Stl	Bl	Pts	ppg
Regular Season	295	3,208	.581	1,602	.546	3,691	716	243	815	6,585	27.2
Playoffs	36	349	.583	213	.511	410	132	29	64	911	25.3
All-Star	4	25	.472	19	.500	34	2	5	8	69	17.3

with and against Wilt Chamberlain and Shaq has the same kind of presence on the court. He's the type of force that opposing players always want to be aware of where he is and what he may try to do next. And he can do an awful lot."

Off the court, O'Neal has become the same kind of marketing phenomena as Michael Jordan. He endorses a wide array of products and already has appeared in a major motion picture. If that's not enough, he is a rap artist with a growing singing career. O'Neal's first album—*Shaq Diesel*—gained critical acclaim and started climbing the record charts from the day it was released.

On the court, the Magic improved from 21 to 41 victories during O'Neal's first season, and to 50 in his second, which O'Neal topped off by being named to the All-NBA Third Team.

Then Orlando and O'Neal really took off. O'Neal won the 1995 scoring title and led the Magic to 57 wins and a berth in the NBA Finals, where Houston proved just too experienced, sweeping Orlando in four games. He played in his third straight All-Star Game and finished runnerup to San Antonio's David Robinson in the NBA MVP balloting.

"He is so big and strong that when you go over to help out on O'Neal you're taking your life into your hands," says team-mate Horace Grant.

O'Neal added a variety of new offensive moves during the 1995–96 season, silencing critics who said his game was one-dimensional. Looking to add even more dimensions to his career, O'Neal left the Magic for the Los Angeles Lakers after the 1995–96 season. The 1996 Dream Team member, who has already made two movies and two rap albums, should be right at home in Hollywood.

> **"I'VE PLAYED WITH MOSES MALONE, DAVID ROBINSON AND KAREEM ABDUL-JABBAR AND I DON'T SAY THIS LIGHTLY, BUT SHAQUILLE'S THE BEST I HAVE EVER PLAYED WITH OR AGAINST."**
>
> **Mark McNamara, former NBA center**

O'Neal's incredible size is matched only by his all-around ability which extends to every corner of the game.

SCOTTIE PIPPEN

Out of the Shadows

• •

There were days growing up in the tiny community of Hamburg, Arkansas, that Scottie Pippen couldn't even play basketball.

• •

It wasn't that there weren't plenty of games going on. It's just that Pippen was considered too small and certainly not good enough to run with his older brothers. So he would stand along the sidelines watching the others play while dribbling a ball and wondering if his time would ever come.

Even as a high school senior, Pippen was a starting guard with a limited future. He stood only 6–1 and not a single college scout came around to watch him play. His high school coach eventually convinced a small local college—Central Arkansas—to give Pippen a job helping out with the team which in turn would help him pay school expenses.

"I was actually a water boy, a manager on my first college team," says Pippen. "No one thought I could play. Then a couple guys quit the team and I think the coach was tired of hearing me beg for an opportunity. He finally gave me a spot on the team."

Four years later, Pippen had grown to 6–7 and every NBA executive in the country wanted Pippen playing for them. Chicago was one of the first teams to catch Pippen's college act. By the time the 1987 NBA Draft rolled around, the Bulls

Scottie Pippen orchestrates the play.

CAREER RECORD

PERSONAL

Birthplace/Date	Hamburg, Arkansas/9.25.65
Height/Weight	6-7/225

AWARDS

MVP	None
All-Star Selections	1990, 1992-96
Finals MVP	None

CAREER

University	Central Arkansas (1983-87)
Pro. Career	9 seasons, Chicago Bulls (1987-96)

PLAYING RECORD	G	FG	Pct	FT	Pct	Reb	Ast	Stl	Bl	Pts	ppg
Regular Season	707	4,975	.486	2,106	.687	4,900	3723	1,538	677	12,490	17.7
Playoffs	138	935	.459	525	.717	1,087	738	241	133	2,499	18.1
All-Star	6	30	.441	10	.625	36	15	17	6	77	12.8

wheeled and dealed to land Pippen.

After a slow start, Pippen developed into one of the league's most versatile players. Those early days as a point guard had provided Pippen with better than average ball-handling skills for a player his size. He could play small forward, substitute for Michael Jordan at shooting guard and, when the Bulls needed a big team on the floor, move over to the point.

By the beginning of the 1990–91 season, Pippen had also developed into one of the league's best defenders. With long arms, unusual quickness, incredible jumping ability and an innate ability to read offenses, Pippen became a defensive force.

"There were times when I felt that Scottie had an even greater potential than Michael," says Bulls assistant coach Tex Winter. "Michael wouldn't agree with that, but Pippen has those long arms and great reaction and he can jump over the moon. Michael could do those things too, but Pippen was a little bigger."

As Pippen developed into a star, the Bulls developed into champions. Pippen was named to the NBA All-Defensive First Team in 1992, 1993, 1994 and 1995 while averaging more than 18 points a game and playing a variety of positions. He also joined Jordan as a member of USA Basketball's 1992 Dream Team.

"For all those years playing with Michael, Scottie Pippen had to accept that in the public's eye no matter how well he might have played, he'd never be better than the second best player in the league," says Bill Walton, a former NBA star. "Other than Michael, who's better? Who does more things? Maybe no one."

"THERE WERE TIMES WHEN I FELT THAT SCOTTIE HAD AN EVEN GREATER POTENTIAL THAN MICHAEL (JORDAN)."

Bulls assistant Tex Winter

Why the black wrist band? To keep Pippen's elbow from hitting the rim on slams like this.

DAVID ROBINSON

The Admiral's in Charge

Nicknamed "The Admiral," David Robinson became an All-America center during his four years at the U.S. Naval Academy.

With extraordinary quickness and finesse for a player his size, the 7–1 Robinson reminded NBA coaches of past greats like Wilt Chamberlain and Bill Russell. In fact, some thought Robinson might eventually be the best of both, combining remarkable defensive skills with an offensive game that included everything from dunks to jump shots.

But San Antonio had to wait two years after using the No. 1 pick in the 1987 NBA Draft to select Robinson. Although his height kept Robinson from many military jobs, he was required to fulfill two years of active duty following his final year of school. Robinson was allowed to play in the 1988 Olympics where he led the men's basketball team to a bronze medal.

"We knew what we were getting," says Bob Bass, who drafted Robinson for San Antonio. "We knew what kind of impact he would make on our ballclub. All you had to do was watch him play. There wasn't anything he couldn't do on a basketball floor."

Even after two years off, Robinson became an instant star. He averaged 24.3

CAREER RECORD

PERSONAL											
Birthplace/Date	Key West, Florida/8.6.65										
Height /Weight	7-1/235										
AWARDS											
MVP	1995										
All-Star Selections	1990-95										
Finals MVP	None										
CAREER											
University	Navy (1983-87)										
Pro. Career	6 seasons, San Antonio Spurs (1989-95 – in military service 1987-89),										

PLAYING RECORD	G	FG	Pct	FT	Pct	Reb	Ast	Stl	Bl	Pts	ppg
Regular Season	557	5,051	.523	4,134	.745	6,563	1,718	934	2,008	14,260	25.6
Playoffs	53	445	.488	382	.728	623	156	67	165	1,273	24.0
All-Star	7	44	.587	30	.667	50	8	11	11	118	16.9

points, 12 rebounds and blocked nearly four shots a game while directing one of the most impressive single-season turn-arounds in NBA history. San Antonio finished 21-61 the year before Robinson arrived. With the Admiral in the middle, the Spurs improved to 56-26 and extended Portland to the seventh game of the Western Conference Semifinals, a game the Trail Blazers won in overtime.

"You look at David Robinson and what is there that he can't do?" says Chicago star Michael Jordan. "He's as fast as any big man in the game, he can block shots better than any player in the league and he can score. If he ever develops a sky-hook like Kareem Abdul-Jabbar did, David Robinson will be unstoppable."

But Robinson's greatest season might have come during the 1994–95 campaign. He averaged more than 28 points and 11 rebounds per game while leading the Spurs to a franchise-record 62 victories. Not surprisingly, Robinson was named the NBA's Most Valuable Player for the first time in his career.

Defensively, Robinson has been a force since his first NBA game. Twice he has led the league in blocked shots. In 1992, Robinson also was named NBA Defensive Player of the Year. During the 1990-91 and 1991-92 seasons, Robinson was a member of the All-NBA First Team and NBA All-Defensive First Team.

And in 1992, Robinson finally got the Olympic gold medal that had eluded the United States in 1988. Robinson was a key member of USA Basketball's Dream Team, as he was again in 1996.

The Admiral: Former U.S. Naval officer David Robinson now directs a floor show in San Antonio; OPPOSITE Jump shots are just part of the repertoire.

"DAVID ROBINSON CAN BE AS GOOD AS HE WANTS TO BE IN THIS GAME. HE HAS EVERYTHING IT TAKES TO BECOME ONE OF THE GREATEST CENTERS TO EVER PLAY THE GAME."

Chuck Daly, Dream Team coach

JOHN STOCKTON

No Passing Fancy

John Stockton has never understood all the fuss. As a high school sophomore, Stockton stood 5–4 and weighed just 115 pounds. That he often destroyed players bigger and stronger on neighborhood basketball courts surprised everyone but Stockton.

Somehow John Stockton knew exactly where he was going. More than anyone else, Stockton knew nothing would get in his way including the pint-size body that housed the spirit of a fighter. But even when the Utah Jazz made Stockton their No. 1 pick in the 1984 Draft, there were skeptics.

How could a player from a small Catholic college called Gonzaga make it in the NBA? And how could anyone standing 6–1 and weighing less than 180 pounds hope to survive the rough and tumble ways of professional basketball?

"I just always thought I could compete," says Stockton simply. "Not that I thought I was better than Magic Johnson or players like that. But I knew I could compete with them."

And that, Utah coach Jerry Sloan will tell you, is exactly why Stockton has become one of the greatest point guards in the history of basketball. Before Stockton only two players had handed out more than 1,000 assists in a season. Isiah Thomas and Kevin Porter each did it one time. Starting with the 1987–88 season, Stockton dished out more than 1,100

Passing Zone: Stockton has become the greatest assist man in NBA history.

CAREER RECORD

PERSONAL	
Birthplace/Date	Spokane, Washington/3.6.62
Height /Weight	6-1/175
AWARDS	
MVP	None
All- Star Selections	1989-96
Finals MVP	None
CAREER	
University	Gonzaga (1980-84)
Pro. Career	12 seasons, Utah Jazz (1984-96)

PLAYING RECORD	G	FG	Pct	FT	Pct	Reb	Ast	Stl	Bl	Pts	ppg
Regular Season	980	4,752	.517	3,222	.832	2,831	11,310	2369	201	13,289	13.6
Playoffs	107	525	.470	383	.818	344	1175	214	34	1,503	14.1
All-Star	8	25	.455	4	.667	17	64	14	1	60	7.5

assists for five straight seasons.

Until Stockton only Boston Celtics great Bob Cousy had won more than three consecutive assists titles. Stockton won his eighth in a row in the 1994–95 season. Until Stockton, superstar Magic Johnson had the highest career average for assists per game with 11.35. Stockton's is at 11.5 and climbing.

The three highest single season assist totals in NBA history belong to Stockton as do the two highest single season averages. He has had 28 assists in one game and twice passed out 11 in a single quarter.

If Stockton were only a remarkable playmaker he would be an All-Star. But Stockton has twice led the NBA in steals, made the NBA All-Defensive Second Team three times, and averaged more than 13 points a game while making 51 percent of his shots, many of those from three-point range.

That's why Stockton has appeared in every All-Star Game since 1989 and he was an easy choice for USA Basketball's 1992 Dream Team.

"A lot of people wonder where this team would be without John Stockton," says teammate and fellow All-Star Karl Malone. "Well, I don't want to find out. He's too good. That's all anyone needs to know."

In 1994–95, Stockton passed Johnson and the NBA's all-time leader in assists and Stockton also became the first man to record 10,000 regular-season assists.

The 1995–96 season found Stockton rewriting another page of the record book by setting a new record for steals in a career. Stockton steered the Jazz to within one win of the NBA Finals, showing he has no intention of slowing down.

"HE DOES SO MANY THINGS SO WELL THAT TO TRY TO COMMENT ON EACH OF THEM WOULD BE TOO MUCH WORK. LET'S PUT IT THIS WAY, HE'S PERFECT—AND HE'S IMPROVING."

Utah Jazz president Frank Layden

Karl Malone scores more, but Stockton remains the Jazz point man.

THE ALL-STAR GAME

It started as an idea. With the NBA trying hard to find its way into the hearts and minds of sports fans, why not gather the league's best players every year for an All-Star Game? In the 33 years between 1951 and 1983, the idea turned into an event as big as any in professional sports. Games were sold out quickly, fans gathered around televisions to watch the proceedings live and players worked to become among the few chosen to participate. Since 1984, the game has been included as part of a gala All-Star Weekend devoted to basketball, complete with additional skill competitions and entertainment for fans of every age.

Nothing mirrors the NBA's dramatic rise more closely than the entertainment spectacle that has become All-Star Weekend.

Once considered an idea that had little chance of working, the NBA All-Star Game has turned into a world-wide event and one of the most successful exhibitions in all of professional sports.

"It's more than a game now," says Detroit Pistons personnel director Billy McKinney. "It's a happening. I remember back in the 1970s when it was a big deal. But even then, the game was nothing like it is now. And it's not just the game. Everything surrounding the game is impressive."

Indeed, the game has merely become the cornerstone of an entertainment-filled weekend.

But it certainly didn't start out that way. Back in 1951, NBA publicist Haskell Cohen had an idea. Why not hold a mid-season classic honoring the league's best players? After all, the NBA was trying to find its place in the sporting landscape. During the 1950–51 season, there were only 11 teams, one of which, Washington, disbanded midway through the season.

But there were also some great players, one of whom was George Mikan, the league's first dominant center and the key to the Minneapolis Lakers. Though the game was growing in popularity, very few people thought that an All-Star Game would prove profitable.

One of those who did, however, was the late Boston Celtics owner Walter Brown. He had not only started to build one of the greatest franchises in league history, but Brown believed in the NBA's future. He also thought an All-Star Game would be a good idea, not only for the league's image but financially as well.

At a time when Brown's own wife was telling him to get out of the basketball business, Brown charged ahead.

"Things were going so badly that even my wife wanted me to get out of the business," said Brown, some years later. "But I thought the All-Star Game would be a good thing. I told the league I would take care of all the expenses and all the losses if there were any.

"Even up until the last week, the game was in doubt. A few days before the game, Maurice Podoloff, the commissioner, called me on the phone and asked me to call it off. He said that everyone he had talked to said it would be a flop, and that the league would look bad." Thanks in part to Brown's perseverance and bravery, the league has never looked better.

The first All-Star Game took place March 2, 1951 in Boston Garden, where 10,094 spectators gathered to see the 20 best basketball players in the league. The Eastern Division romped to an easy 111–94 victory.

AT&T Long Distance Shootout Champions

1986 —	Larry Bird, Boston
1987 —	Larry Bird, Boston
1988 —	Larry Bird, Boston
1989 —	Dale Ellis, Seattle
1990 —	Craig Hodges, Chicago
1991 —	Craig Hodges, Chicago
1992 —	Craig Hodges, Chicago
1993 —	Mark Price, Cleveland
1994 —	Mark Price, Cleveland
1995 —	Glen Rice, Miami
1996 —	Tim Legler, Washington

Nestlé Slam-Dunk Champions

1984 — Larry Nance, Phoenix
1985 — Dominique Wilkins, Atlanta
1986 — Spud Webb, Atlanta
1987 — Michael Jordan, Chicago
1988 — Michael Jordan, Chicago
1989 — Kenny Walker, New York
1990 — Dominique Wilkins, Atlanta
1991 — Dee Brown, Boston
1992 — Cedric Ceballos, Phoenix
1993 — Harold Miner, Miami
1994 — Isaiah Rider, Minnesota
1996 — Brent Barry, L.A. Clippers

THE SELECTION PROCESS

In the years since, the game has become a glowing example of the NBA's influence and popularity. As creative as the players themselves, league executives have turned a simple game into a weekend that starts gathering momentum just weeks into the regular season.

The process itself has become part of the show. Ballots are made available to fans attending games around the league. Fans are asked to vote for five players—two guards, two forwards and a center—they want to see starting for the Eastern Conference and Western Conference squads. Players receiving the most votes then occupy the five starting positions on each team for the All-Star Game.

Reserves are chosen by the respective head coaches. The coaches are determined by regular season records. The coach of the team with the best record in each conference through the first three months of the current season earns the right to coach that conference's All-Star team.

But that's only part of the All-Star Weekend fun. In 1984, as the league exploded in world-wide popularity, events surrounding the game were added to satisfy demand. Not only were All-Star Games now played before sellout crowds in huge arenas, but media coverage turned the game into one of the country's most

anticipated sporting events.

Indeed, reporters from around the world cover the event with the game televised around the globe. And no one, it seems, ever goes away disappointed. Thanks in large part to the players and coaches, the floor often seems more like a stage. Not only are the game's best players more rested, but they are surrounded by stars at every position. The result is usually a high-scoring game revolving around an array of slick passes, slam dunks and long-range jumpers.

The league, responding to the overwhelming popularity of the game, created All-Star Weekend. The first Nestlé Slam-Dunk Championship was held in 1984 at Indiana along with the first Schick Legends Classic (replaced in 1994 by the Schick Rookie Classic). In 1986, the AT&T Long Distance Shootout was instituted.

All-Star Saturday immediately became as popular, as some of the league's biggest stars competed head-to-head. Boston's Larry Bird won the first three AT&T Long Distance Shootouts. Players shoot from five positions in a set time period. The player who makes the most shots advances until two are left in the finals.

Chicago's Michael Jordan and Atlanta's Dominique Wilkins each won a pair of Slam Dunk titles, with Jordan winning the 1987 event in Seattle by taking off from the free-throw line and sailing toward the basket before dunking. Although the format has changed over the years, dunkers are scored on their dunking ability and creativity.

But the All-Star Game remains the primary attraction. Players are allowed to show all their moves and reach deep into their bags of tricks. There are spectacular dunks, remarkable passes and just enough defense and shotblocking to produce a spectacular show.

And just as Walter Brown predicted back in 1951, the All-Star Game has become the showcase for the greatest basketball players in the world.

Boston Celtics sharpshooter Larry Bird won the first three AT&T Long Distance Shootouts.

THE NBA DRAFT

The evolution of the NBA Draft has matched that of the league itself. In the early days, teams gathered around a table in their offices and called off the names of the players selected on a conference call as an official at the league's New York headquarters recorded the information. Few teams did extensive scouting. In the years since, however, the draft has become one of the NBA's biggest shows. Every team studies films, scouting reports and pages of vital information on players from all over the world. The draft itself is now an internationally televised event with 20,000 fans or more packing arenas every year to watch the future unfold.

No one event can change the direction of a franchise like the NBA Draft. In the early years as the league evolved, luck and intuition filled the void for teams that didn't have either the money or personnel to scout college players.

In 1955, Leonard Koppett, a veteran basketball writer, described that year's draft session in a column for the New York Post. According to Koppett, NBA Commissioner Maurice Podoloff sat at the head of a table and called off the names of the league's nine teams.

"Since it is a relatively small family in the NBA, with everyone on quite friendly terms these days, there's a good deal of kidding," wrote Koppett.

"So when Fort Wayne's Charley Eckman chose Dick Howard, Boston's Red Auerbach quipped, 'Is that a relative, Charley?'

"'Wife's cousin,' Eckman shot back."

The atmosphere has changed considerably since. In fact, the entire process has changed dramatically just in the last 10 years.

"Back then teams didn't even have full-time scouts," says Chicago Bulls vice president of operations, Jerry Krause. "You were lucky if you had an assistant coach much less a scout. No one had the things

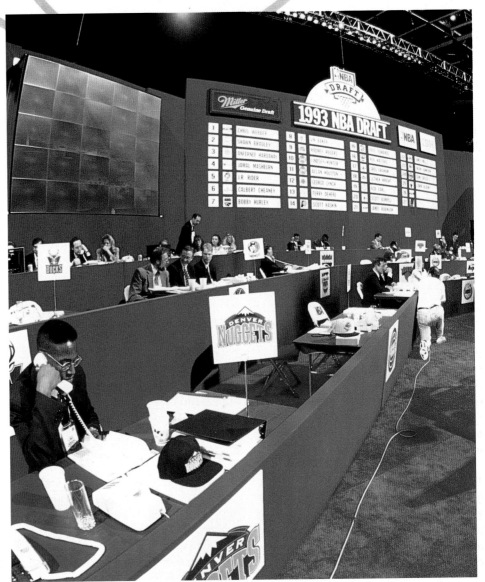

Team officials prepare for the 1993 NBA Draft at the Palace of Auburn Hills in Michigan.

that are available today. But that didn't mean you couldn't find players. You just had to dig a little more that's all."

Since the beginning, however, the draft has had a very simple mission: to promote competitive balance throughout the league. Teams selected in inverse order of their regular-season records. Thus, the weakest teams were awarded the first shot at available new talent.

In the hope of solidifying franchises, early teams were also allowed a "territorial pick." Each team could select one player from its geographic area to maintain local interest in the professional team.

Over the years, however, territorial picks were eliminated. In 1966, the coin flip was introduced to determine the No. 1 pick in the draft. The idea was to maintain integrity in the game since the team with the worst record wouldn't be guaranteed of landing the first choice.

In some cases the coin flip changed the fortunes of entire franchises. In 1969, the Milwaukee Bucks won a coin flip with Phoenix and ended up with Kareem Abdul-Jabbar. Two years later, the Bucks won an NBA championship. Ten years later, the Los Angeles Lakers flipped with Chicago and won the right to choose first. The Lakers selected Earvin "Magic" Johnson and in 1980 won the first of five NBA titles. Phoenix still hasn't won a championship while Chicago didn't win its first until 1991.

THE LOTTERY

To completely take away any incentive a poor team might have for losing games and thus getting into the coin flip, the league instituted the NBA Draft Lottery in 1985. Initially the lottery was used to determine the order of selection for non-playoff teams or the teams owning those picks through trades. The Lottery determined the order for the first round only, and the order for subsequent rounds went in inverse order of regular season records.

The process was further refined for the 1990 NBA Draft. The Lottery, which included 11 teams due to expansion, was weighted to favor the worst teams. The team with the worst record had 11 chances to land the No. 1 pick. The second worst team had 10 chances and so on.

For the 1994 NBA Draft, the lottery sys-

tem was modified yet again. Ironically, the incredible luck of the Orlando Magic led to the most recent change. Orlando gained the No. 1 pick in 1992 and selected 7–1 center Shaquille O'Neal. In 1993, the Magic finished just one game out of the playoffs. As a lottery team, Orlando had the lowest odds of gaining the top pick again. But it happened. The Magic had back-to-back No. 1 picks.

In an attempt to further improve the odds for the league's worst teams, the new lottery system increases the chance of the team with the worst record getting the top pick from 16.7 percent to 25 percent.

Two other key changes over the years involved players and the length of the draft. Prior to 1971, players could not be drafted into the NBA until their college classes had graduated. In other words, a college junior was not eligible to play in the NBA. That changed when Spencer Haywood filed a lawsuit against the league for refusing to allow him to enter the draft before the expiration of his collegiate eligibility. A year later, underclassmen who demonstrated financial hardship were allowed into the draft. In 1976, the draft was opened to all players with or without financial hardship. To become eligible for the draft, underclassmen had to renounce their remaining eligibility in a letter to the commissioner 45 days prior to the draft. That rule remains in place today.

The length of the draft has changed dramatically as well. After years with no limits to the number of rounds, the league

instituted a 10-round draft in 1974. In other words, each team had 10 opportunities to select players.

The draft was reduced to seven rounds in 1985, three rounds in 1988 and the present two rounds in 1989. Those changes, along with the booming popularity of college basketball and professional game, have turned the NBA Draft into a major international media event.

BUCKS LAND BIG DOG

The 1994 NBA Draft was held the Hoosier Dome in Indianapolis where more than 19,000 fans came to see one of their own steal the show. Virtually all of the top picks, including crowd favorite and the No. 1 selection, Glenn "Big Dog" Robinson from nearby Purdue University, were on hand and were all introduced by the commissioner upon being chosen.

The Milwaukee Bucks won the Lottery jackpot and selected Robinson.

Since draft picks can be traded between teams, the NBA Draft has become one of the league's most important offseason events.

As teams now have entire departments devoted to scouting players, complete with state-of-the-art video equipment and large travel budgets, the NBA Draft is a bigger event than ever.

HITTING THE LOTTERY JACKPOT

YEAR	TEAM	FIRST PLAYER CHOSEN
1985	New York	Patrick Ewing
1986	Cleveland	Brad Daugherty
1987	San Antonio	David Robinson
1988	Los Angeles Clippers	Danny Manning
1989	Sacramento	Pervis Ellison
1990	New Jersey	Derrick Coleman
1991	Charlotte	Larry Johnson
1992	Orlando	Shaquille O'Neal
1993	Orlando	Chris Webber
1994	Milwaukee	Glenn Robinson
1995	Golden State	Joe Smith
1996	Philadelphia	Allen Iverson

THE NBA GOES GLOBAL

For much of its existence, the NBA remained an American enterprise. But now, with television contracts in more than 160 countries and offices around the world, the league is beginning to make the NBA experience an international one. It started with the McDonald's Championship, an international tournament that featured one NBA team. Now there are 3-on-3 World Tours sponsored in part by Converse, NBA players competing in the Olympic Games and the World Championship of Basketball, expansion to Canada, regular season games played in Japan, and the biennial McDonald's Championship now features the NBA Champion against other club champions from around the world.

NBA Commissioner David Stern remembers the request. He was talking to members of the Chinese government during a trip to China. One of them turned to Stern and asked if he would bring the Red Oxen to China.

Stern understood.

"They wanted to see the Chicago Bulls," recalls Stern. "They wanted to know if we could put together a game in China that would include the Bulls."

There had been other requests from inside the former Soviet Union, Japan, South America and virtually every European country. Thanks to Stern's marketing genius and the basketball genius of the NBA players, interest in the NBA game extended around the globe.

"Sports really is the international language," says Stern. "And we think basketball is up there on top of the list in terms of dialect."

In the Yokohama Arena in Japan, where the Portland Trail Blazers and Los Angeles Clippers opened the 1994–95 season with two games, one Japanese fan shaved the sides of his head and used red and black marking pens to write "Go Drexler."

Indeed, the NBA presence now spans the globe. During the 1994–95 preseason, more than 38,000 fans poured into the Palacio de los Deportes in Mexico City for a four-game exhibition tournament that included the Houston Rockets, San Antonio Spurs, Seattle SuperSonics and the Los Angeles Clippers. There were also exhibition games in Europe, with the Golden State Warriors and Charlotte Hornets hooking up in Paris.

And that's just the beginning. More than 50 countries carried the 1994 NBA Finals between Houston and New York live. Meanwhile, the global distribution of NBA games for the 1995–96 season included more than 160 countries and access to more than 400 million households worldwide. The NBA, with offices in Switzerland, Hong Kong and Australia, added one in Tokyo in 1994 and another in Miami to provide service for Latin America.

And in 1995, the NBA champion will compete in the McDonald's Championship to be played in the London Arena with some of the best club teams from around the world.

Though the momentum had been building for years, it got a big boost during the 1992 Barcelona Olympics when USA Basketball's Dream Team stole the international show.

Larry Johnson poses in front of the Eiffel Tower.

"Since the impressive performance of the Dream Team at the Olympics, basketball has gained unprecedented worldwide attention, especially among young people," says Stern.

New York's Patrick Ewing explains the finer points of dribbling to a child on the NBA's Goodwill of Africa in 1994.

One grassroots example of the international lure of basketball was the overwhelming response to the 1994 Converse/NBA 3-on-3 World Tour. The event matches teams of three players each in a variety of age, size and skill levels. The games are usually played outdoors, which make it one of the largest spectator events in Europe.

The 1994 Tour stopped in 24 cities, attracting more than 43,000 players and more than 750,000 spectators. And it will only get bigger. In 1995, the event expanded to 28 cities in 11 countries with expectations of more than a million spectators.

Stern has also made a commitment to the continent of Africa. During the summer of 1994, NBA players and coaches combined on clinics in Cape Town and Johannesburg with an additional stop in Soweto. When the NBA contingent arrived in Soweto, they found hundreds of youngsters waiting for them. "This trip demonstrates first hand the ability of sports to serve as a vehicle for the exchange of ideas on a global basis," says Stern.

The United States entry in the 16-team World Championship of Basketball, that was played in Toronto and Hamilton, Ontario, Canada in August, 1994, resembled the overwhelming performance of the original Dream Team in Barcelona.

But more than anything else, the location turned out to be a fitting one. In 1994, Toronto and Vancouver became the league's 28th and 29ths franchises. Both began with the 1995–96 season. Why Canada? That's easy, according to Stern, who pointed out that a country of 28 million potential sports fans presented a spectacular opportunity for the NBA, and Toronto and Vancouver represented natural East-West rivals that should help the sport get off to a fast start.

With Canada on board, could Mexico be next? The success of the annual preseason games in Mexico City could be a portent of things to come. And don't forget the NBA's recent trips to Japan, where teams have played regular season games. "No question," says former Lakers star Magic Johnson. "People love the NBA game."

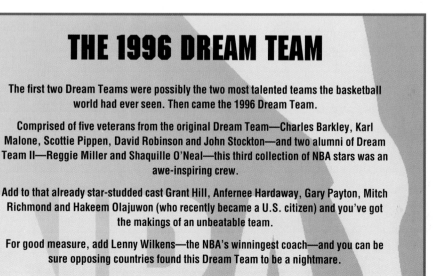

THE 1996 DREAM TEAM

The first two Dream Teams were possibly the two most talented teams the basketball world had ever seen. Then came the 1996 Dream Team.

Comprised of five veterans from the original Dream Team—Charles Barkley, Karl Malone, Scottie Pippen, David Robinson and John Stockton—and two alumni of Dream Team II—Reggie Miller and Shaquille O'Neal—this third collection of NBA stars was an awe-inspiring crew.

Add to that already star-studded cast Grant Hill, Anfernee Hardaway, Gary Payton, Mitch Richmond and Hakeem Olajuwon (who recently became a U.S. citizen) and you've got the makings of an unbeatable team.

For good measure, add Lenny Wilkens—the NBA's winningest coach—and you can be sure opposing countries found this Dream Team to be a nightmare.

GLOSSARY OF TERMS

Airball: When a player shoots a shot that doesn't touch the rim it is sarcastically referred to as an "airball."

Alley-oop pass: The pass is thrown as a player runs toward the basket. The receiving player catches the ball in the air and either dunks or lays it in the hoop without touching the ground.

Assist: A player earns an assist when his pass to another player leads directly to a basket.

Backcourt: As it refers to players, backcourt generally means guards. A team with a great backcourt would have two very talented guards.

Bench: Where substitutes and coaches reside during games. A "bench" player is another term for a reserve.

Bounce pass: Passing the ball from one player to another by bouncing it on the floor.

Center: Usually the tallest player on a team's starting unit with a variety of skills that sometimes include shotblocking, rebounding and scoring. New York's Patrick Ewing, San Antonio's David Robinson, Orlando's Shaquille O'Neal and Charlotte's Alonzo Mourning are examples of top-flight centers.

Draft: A selection process to determine on which NBA teams the top newcomers will play.

Dunk: The act of slamming the ball through the basket with one or two hands.

Fast break: A play that occurs when the offensive team quickly gets the ball out ahead of the defensive team. The offensive team usually has a one or two-man advantage as it goes in for a score.

Field goal: Either a two-point or three-point basket can also be referred to as a field goal.

Foul: A violation commited by one player against another player. After accumulating six personal fouls in a game, a player is disqualifed for the rest of the game.

Free throw: When a foul is commited, the player fouled usually gets to take two shots from the free-throw line which is 15 feet from the basket. The free throws are worth one point each.

Frontcourt: As it refers to players, frontcourt usually means forwards and centers.

Halftime: The time in between the first half and the second half. Each half consists of two 12-minute quarters. Teams break between the second and third quarters and change the baskets at which they shoot.

Jump shot: A shot taken away from the basket. Players usually jump into the air, set themselves and take the shot. Sometimes referred to as a "jumper."

Lane: The painted area running from the end line under the basket out to the free-throw line. Offensive players can not be in the lane more than three seconds.

Lottery: The process that determines the order of selection at the start of the NBA Draft.

Overtime: When a game is tied at the end of regulation play the two teams play a five-minute overtime period. A game can include as many overtime periods as are necessary to determine a winner.

Paint: The area under the basket, and extending to the foul line. Also called the "lane," it is always painted a different color from the rest of the floor.

Pivot: This takes place when a player who is holding the ball steps and turns once or more than once in any direction with the same foot, while the other foot — called the pivot foot — is being kept at its point of contact on the floor.

Point guard: Usually a team's primary ballhandler. He leads the offense and distributes the ball to the team's best scorers. Phoenix's Kevin Johnson, Orlando's Anfernee Hardaway, Utah's John Stockton and Seattle's Gary Payton are some of the league's best point guards.

Power forward: Usually occupies one of two forward spots on a five-man unit. Known primarily for their rebounding and defensive skills. Utah's Karl Malone, Chicago's Horace Grant and Portland's Buck Williams are examples of power forwards.

Quadruple-double: Refers to a player who accumulates ten or more in at last four of five statistical categories—points, rebounds, steals, blocked shots, assists—in a single game. Through the 1995–96 season, there have been only four quadruple-doubles in NBA history.

Rebound: The gathering or controlling of a missed shot.

Screen: This is a legal action of a player who, without causing undue contact, delays or prevents an opponent from reaching a desired position.

Shot clock: The 24-second clock used to time possessions. The offensive team has 24 seconds in which to get off a shot.

Shooting guard: Occupies one of two guard positions and usually is one of the team's primary offensive weapons. Chicago Bulls star Michael Jordan is a shooting guard. Others include Indiana's Reggie Miller, Cleveland's Dan Majerle, Golden State's Latrell Sprewell and New York's John Starks.

Sixth man: Usually refers to a team's top reserve.

Small forward: Occupies one of two forward spots, the small forward is most often known for his scoring. Though not necessarily smaller in size, these players are better known for shooting and scoring skills than rebounding or defensive skills. The Los Angeles Clippers' Dominique Wilkins and Chicago's Scottie Pippen are considered small forwards.

Steal: The action of a defensive player in either taking the ball away from an offensive player or intercepting a pass is known as a steal.

Technical foul: Assessed for a number of violations including fighting, verbal abuse of a referee, a second illegal defense call and flagrant foul.

Triple-double: Refers to a player who accumulates double figures, 10 or more, in at least three of five statistical categories—points, rebounds, steals, blocked shots, assists—in a single game.

Turnover: A play that results in a change of possession with the control of the ball going from one team to the other.

BASKETBALL HALL OF FAME

B y 1968, the basketball Hall of Fame was an idea whose time was long overdue. Though a memorial had been agreed upon following the 1939 death of Dr. James Naismith, the game's creator, it took nearly 30 years to make the dream a reality.

The Naismith Memorial Basketball Hall of Fame came alive on February 18, 1968, on the Springfield College campus in Springfield, Mass. In 1985 a modern, three-level structure was built on the banks of the Connecticut River in downtown Springfield, the town where Dr. Naismith first tossed a round ball through a peach basket in 1891.

The Hall of Fame recognizes basketball at every level from high school to the Olympics, amateur and professional. An Honors Committee, composed of 24 members representing various levels of basketball, votes each year on nominees, who need 18 votes to be elected to the Hall of Fame. The first Hall of Fame elections were held in 1959, nine years before a building even existed. Since then there have been coaches, players and individual contributors enshrined as well as four teams.

Two of the most unique individuals are John Wooden and Bill Bradley. Wooden was named as a player in 1960 and as a coach in 1972. Bradley, who played for the New York Knicks, is a United States Senator and was inducted in 1982.

The following are brief biographies of all NBA-related players in the Hall of Fame:

Nate "Tiny" Archibald is the only player to lead the league in scoring and assists in the same season.

Kareem Abdul-Jabbar: 7–2, 267-pound center; born April 16, 1947, formerly known as Lew Alcindor. Attended UCLA; played 20 seasons with Milwaukee Bucks and Los Angeles Lakers. Holds NBA record for seasons, games and minutes played, also points scored, field goals (made and attempted) and blocked shots. Also set single-season record for defensive rebounds (1,111 in 1975–76). Named NBA MVP six times, and 18 times an All-Star.

Nate (Tiny) Archibald: 6–1, 160-pound guard; born April 18, 1948. Attended Arizona Western and Texas-El Paso; played 13 seasons with four teams. Was first player to lead NBA in scoring (34.0) and assists (11.4) in the same season (1973–74). A six-time All-Star.

Paul Arizin: 6–4, 200-pound forward; born April 9, 1928. Attended Villanova; played 10 seasons with Philadelphia. One of the highest scoring players of his era, from 1950 through the end of 1961–62 season. Nine times an All-Star.

Rick Barry: 6–7, 205-pound forward; born March 28, 1944. Attended Miami. Played 14 professional seasons, 10 of those in the NBA. One of basketball's greatest scorers and shooters. A career 90 percent free-throw shooter, utilizing a distinctive underhanded shooting style. Seven-time All-Star.

Elgin Baylor: 6–5, 225-pound forward; born September 16, 1934. Attended College of Idaho and University of Seattle. Played 14 seasons with the Minneapolis and Los Angeles Lakers. Averaged more than 34 points a game for three straight years in the 1960s. 11-time All-Star.

Rochester's Bob Davies was one of the first great shooting guards.

Walt Bellamy: 6–10½, 245-pound center; born July 24, 1939. Attended Indiana; played 14 seasons with six teams. Bellamy averaged career highs of 31.6 points and 19.0 in his rookie season. Four-time All-Star.

Dave Bing: 6–3, 180-pound guard; born November 24, 1943. Attended Syracuse. Bing played 12 seasons for three teams; led the league in scoring (27.1) in 1967–68. Seven-time All-Star.

Bill Bradley: 6–5, 205-pound forward; born July 28, 1943. Attended Princeton. A Rhodes Scholar, Bradley keyed the Knicks' glory days in the 1960s and early 1970s. Became a U.S. Senator. One All-Star Game.

Al Cervi: 5–11½, 155-pound guard; born February 12, 1917. Did not attend college. Nicknamed "Digger," Cervi started professional career in 1937. In military service from 1938 to 1945. Cervi finished his NBA career with Syracuse at age of 36. One of the great early guards, he retired before the All-Star Game was instituted.

Wilt Chamberlain: 7–1, 275-pound center; born August 21, 1936. Attended Kansas. A.k.a. "Wilt the Stilt" and "the Big Dipper," Chamberlain is one of the greatest scorers in NBA history, and the only player to score 100 points in an NBA game. Averaged 50.4 points one season (1961–62) and had 30.1 career average. Played 14 years with three teams. 13-time All-Star.

Bob Cousy: 6–1½, 175-pound point guard; born August 9, 1928. Attended Holy Cross. One of the more dazzling ballhandlers in NBA history, Cousy played 13 seasons for the Boston Celtics and finished career with Cincinnati. Set NBA record leading league in assists eight straight seasons. An All-Star 13 times.

Billy Cunningham: 6–6, 220-pound forward; born June 3, 1943. Attended North Carolina. Played nine NBA seasons with Philadelphia and two in the ABA. Four-time NBA All-Star and legendary leaper. Cunningham could do everything from rebounding to scoring.

Bob Davies: 6–1, 175-pound guard; born January 15, 1920. Attended Franklin & Marshall and Seton Hall. Davies' professional career started in 1946. Played 10 years with Rochester as a scoring guard. Played in the first four All-Star Games.

Julius (Dr. J) Erving: 6–6½, 200-pound forward; born February 22, 1950. Attended Massachusetts. One of the most acrobatic and creative players in NBA history, Erving became known as "Dr. J." Started in the ABA before finishing career with Philadelphia. An All-Star every one of his 16 professional seasons.

Walt (Clyde) Frazier: 6–4, 200-pound guard; born March 29, 1945. Attended Southern Illinois. Cool and calm on the floor, Frazier was one of the most versatile guards of his era. Played 13 NBA seasons, the first 10 with New York where he led the Knicks to two championships. A seven-time All-Star.

Joe Fulks: 6–5, 190-pound forward; born October 26, 1921. Attended Millsaps and Murray State. Known as "Jumpin' Joe," Fulks played eight seasons with Philadelphia. One of professional basketball's greatest scorers in the late 1940s. A two-time All-Star.

Harry Gallatin: 6–6, 215-pound forward/center; born April 26, 1927. Attended Northeast Missouri. Played 10 years, nine with New York. A brilliant rebounder, Gallatin was nicknamed "the Horse." A seven-time All-Star.

George Gervin: 6–7, 185-pound guard; born April 27, 1952. Attended Eastern Michigan. Known as "The Iceman," Gervin was one of the great shooting guards ever to play the game. Deadly with a jump shot or his finger-roll lay-ups, Gervin averaged 26.2 points over his career, led the NBA in scoring four times and holds the record for most points in a single quarter—33.

Gail Goodrich: 6–1, 175-pound guard; born April 23, 1943. Attended UCLA. Goodrich played 14 NBA seasons, earning five All-Star appearances. Goodrich was a starter on the 1972 Los Angeles Lakers team that won the NBA Championship. Goodrich averaged 18.6 points over his career.

Tom Gola: 6–6, 205-pound forward; born January 13, 1933. Attended LaSalle. Played 10 seasons with three teams. A versatile player with size, Gola helped make Philadelphia a consistent playoff team from the mid-1950s to the early 1960s. A four-time All-Star.

Hal Greer: 6–2, 175-pound guard; born June 26, 1936. Attended Marshall. A brilliant scoring guard, Greer played 15 NBA seasons, the last 10 with Philadelphia. Averaged more than 20 points a game first seven seasons in Philadephia. A 10-time All-Star.

Cliff Hagan: 6–4, 215-pound forward; born December 9, 1931. Attended Kentucky. A great scorer, Hagan led St. Louis to the 1958 championship. Finished his professional career in the ABA. A four-time All-Star.

John Havlicek: 6–5, 205-pound forward/guard; born April 8, 1940. Attended Ohio State. Brilliant in every phase of the game, Havlicek played on Boston teams that won eight championships. Nicknamed "Hondo," he was drafted by professional football's Cleveland Browns. A 13-time All-Star.

Connie Hawkins: 6–8, 215-pound forward; born July 17, 1942. Attended Iowa, but left after freshman year to join ABL. After a period out of professional basketball and two ABA seasons, Hawkins joined Phoenix in 1969. Considered one of the greatest pure talents in history. An All-Star four times.

Elvin Hayes: 6–9, 235-pound forward/center; born November 17, 1945. Attended Houston. Missed just nine games in his 16-year career. As great a scorer as he was a rebounder, Hayes helped Washington to the 1978 title. A 12-time All-Star.

Tommy Heinsohn: 6–7, 218-pound forward; born August 26, 1934. Attended Holy Cross. A rugged scorer and rebounder, Heinsohn helped Boston to eight titles in nine-year career. Later coached the Celtics to two championships. A five-time All-Star.

Dan Issel: 6–9, 240-pound forward; born October 25, 1948. Attended Kentucky. Played first six professional seasons in ABA, the last nine with Denver Nuggets. A great shooter and rebounder, Issel averaged more than 21 points a game 11 times. Seven-time All-Star.

Harry (Buddy) Jeannette: 5–11, 175-pound guard; born September 15, 1929. Attended Washington & Jefferson. One of the game's top guards in the late 1930s and 1940s. Won four MVP awards and four championships in two leagues.

Neil Johnston: 6–8, 215-pound forward/center; born February 4, 1929. Attended Ohio State. One of his era's greatest scorers, Johnston averaged more than 22 points a game five straight seasons for Philadelphia in the 1950s. Played minor league baseball. Six-time All-Star.

K.C. Jones: 6–1, 200-pound guard; born May 25, 1932. Attended San Francisco. A defensive specialist, Jones played with Bill Russell in college and then at Boston. Helped lead the Celtics to eight championships in his nine NBA seasons. Later became a highly successful NBA coach.

Sam Jones: 6–4, 205-pound guard, born June 24, 1933. Attended North Carolina College. A key to the Boston dynasty, Jones averaged 17.5 points during 12-year career. Member of 10 championship teams in Boston. Five-time All-Star.

Bob Lanier: 6–11, 260-pound center; born September 10, 1948. Attended St.

Bonaventure. One of the greatest centers in NBA history, Lanier played 14 seasons with Detroit and Milwaukee. Averaged more than 20 points a game eight straight seasons. Eight-time All-Star.

Clyde Lovellette: 6–9. 235-pound foward; born September 7, 1929. Attended Kansas. Helped Minneapolis to 1954 title as rookie. Solid scorer and rebounder. Played 11 seasons winning two more championships with Boston. Three-time All-Star.

Pete Maravich: 6–5, 200-pound guard; born June 22, 1947. Attended Lousiana State. Nicknamed "Pistol Pete" for his extraordinary shooting and scoring skills, he was a veritable ballhandling marvel. Averaged 24.2 points during a 10-year career. Four-time All-Star.

Slater Martin: 5–10, 170-pound guard; born October 22, 1925. Attended Texas. Member of Minneapolis teams that won four championships. Later helped lead St. Louis to 1958 title. A seven-time All-Star.

Dick McGuire: 6–0, 180-pound guard; born January 25, 1926. Attended St. John's and Dartmouth. One of the great early point guards. McGuire was nicknamed "Tricky Dick" for his ballhandling and passing skills. Seven-time All-Star.

George Mikan: 6–10½, 245-pound center; born June 18, 1924. Attended DePaul. The first dominant center in professional basketball history, Mikan led the Minneapolis Lakers to five championships. The greatest scorer of his era, Mikan averaged 23.1 pointsover his seven-year NBA career, nine seasons in total. Four-time All-Star.

"Pistol" Pete Maravich drives to another score.

Earl Monroe: 6–3¹/₂, 185-pound guard; born November 21, 1944. Attended Winston-Salem State. One of the flashiest guards ever, Monroe was known as Earl "the Pearl" for his smooth moves. Played on New York title team in 1973. Four-time All-Star.

Calvin Murphy: 5–9, 165-pound guard; born May 9, 1948. Attended Niagara. One of the greatest small players in league history, Murphy could score, pass and shoot as well as anyone in his era. One of the best free-throw shooters (89.2 percent) in history. Played 13 seasons, all with Rockets. Appeared in one All-Star Game.

Bob Pettit: 6–9, 215-pound forward; born December 12, 1932. Attended Louisiana State. A brilliant scorer, Pettit never averaged less than 20.4 points during 11-year career. Sixth highest career scoring average (26.4) in history. An 11-time All-Star.

Andy Phillip: 6–2¹/₂, 195-pound guard/forward; born March 7, 1922. Attended Illinois. Professional career started in 1947. Played on 1957 Boston Celtics championship team. Five-time All-Star.

Jim Pollard: 6–3¹/₂, 190-pound forward; born July 9, 1922. Attended Stanford. Known as for his jumping ability, Pollard helped lead Minneapolis to five championships. Four-time All-Star.

Frank Ramsey: 6–3, 190-pound guard/forward; born July 13, 1931. Attended Kentucky. A key contributor to seven Boston championships, Ramsey shot better than 80 percent from the foul line. One of basketball's best "sixth men" ever.

Willis Reed: 6–9¹/₂, 235-pound center; born June 25, 1942. Attended Grambling. A gifted shooter and defender despite his size, Reed led the New York Knicks to two championships. Spent 10-year career with Knicks. A seven-time All-Star.

Oscar Robertson: 6–5, 210-pound guard; born November 24, 1938. Attended Cincinnati. Played 13 seasons with Cincinnati Royals and Milwaukee Bucks. Until Michael Jordan, Robertson was considered the greatest all-around guard. Averaged a stunning 30.8 points, 11.4 assists and 12.5 rebounds during 1961-62 season. A 12-time All-Star.

Bill Russell: 6–9¹/₂, 220-pound center; born February 12, 1934. Attended San Francisco. Led the Boston Celtics to 11 championships during 13-year playing career, all with the Celtics. Averaged incredible 22.6 rebounds a game during his career. A 12-time All-Star.

Dolph Schayes: 6–8, 220-pound forward; born May 19, 1928. Attended New York University. Great at virtually every aspect of the game, Schayes could rebound, score and shoot as well as any player in his era. Played 16 seasons, 15 with Syracuse. An 11-time All-Star.

Bill Sharman: 6–1, 190-pound guard; born May 25, 1926. Attended University of Southern California. One of Boston's key offensive threats during the 1950s and early 1960s. Played on four championship teams. A career 88.3 percent free-throw shooter. Played minor league baseball. Eight-time All-Star.

David Thompson: 6–4, 180-pound guard; born July 13, 1954. Attended North Carolina State. Thompson, one of the most electrifying leapers ever to play the game, was an All-Star four times for the Denver Nuggets. Thompson owns the third highest point total in a single game in NBA history, scoring 73 against Detroit in 1978.

Nate Thurmond: 6–11, 230-pound center; born July 25, 1941. Attended Bowling Green. A solid, if not dominant big man during the 1960s and early 1970s, Thurmond could score, rebound and block shots. Five-time All-Star.

Jack Twyman: 6–6, 210-pound forward; born May 11, 1934. Attended Cincinnati. Played nine of 11 seasons in Cincinnati. One of the era's top scoring forwards, averaged 31.2 points during 1959–60 season. Six-time All-Star.

Wes Unseld: 6–7½, 245-pound center; born March 14, 1946. Attended Louisville. Named Rookie of the Year and Most Valuable Player during 1968–69 season. Spent entire 13-year career with Bullets franchise. A five-time All-Star.

Bill Walton: 6–11, 235-pound center; born November 5, 1952. Attended UCLA. One of the greatest college players ever. Walton led Portland to the 1977 title and helped Boston to 1986 championship. His career was cut short

by chronic foot injuries (played in only 14 games in four seasons 1978–82). Played in one All-Star Game.

Bobby Wanzer: 6–0, 172-pound guard; born June 4, 1921. Attended Colgate and Seton Hall. Played 10 years with Rochester. A great free-throw shooter, Wanzer developed into a reliable scorer while leading the Rochester offense to 1951 NBA title. Five-time All-Star.

Jerry West: 6–2¹/₂, 180-pound guard; born May 28, 1938. Attended West Virginia. One of the greatest shooting guards in history, West averaged 27.0 points during his 14-year career. He teamed up with Wilt Chamberlain to lead Los Angeles to the 1972 NBA championship. A 12-time All-Star.

Lenny Wilkens: 6–1, 185-pound guard; born October 28, 1937. Attended Providence. One of the game's smartest point guards, Wilkens started his coaching career while still a full-time player. Won 900th game in January 1994. An All-Star nine times during his 15-year career.

George Yardley: 6–5, 195-pound forward; born November 23, 1928. Attended Stanford. In seven NBA seasons, Yardley was named to the All-Star team six times. Yardley became the first NBA player to score 2,000 points in a single season, doing so in 1957–58 for the Detroit Pistons.